Practice the Canadian Firefighter Exam

Practice Test Questions for the
Canadian Firefighter Exam

COMPLETE
TEST PREPARATION INC.
WWW.TEST-PREPARATION.CA

Copyright © 2015 by Complete Test Preparation Inc. ALL RIGHTS RESERVED. No part of this book may be reproduced or transferred in any form or by any means, graphic, electronic, or mechanical, including photocopying, recording, web distribution, taping, or by any information storage retrieval system, without the written permission of the author.

Notice: Complete Test Preparation Inc. makes every reasonable effort to obtain from reliable sources accurate, complete, and timely information about the tests covered in this book. Nevertheless, changes can be made in the tests or the administration of the tests at any time and Complete Test Preparation Inc. makes no representation or warranty, either expressed or implied as to the accuracy, timeliness, or completeness of the information contained in this book. Complete Test Preparation Inc. makes no representations or warranties of any kind, express or implied, about the completeness, accuracy, reliability, suitability or availability with respect to the information contained in this document for any purpose. Any reliance you place on such information is therefore strictly at your own risk.

The author(s) shall not be liable for any loss incurred as a consequence of the use and application, directly or indirectly, of any information presented in this work. Sold with the understanding, the author(s) is not engaged in rendering professional services or advice. If advice or expert assistance is required, the services of a competent professional should be sought.

The company, product and service names used in this publication are for identification purposes only. All trademarks and registered trademarks are the property of their respective owners. Complete Test Preparation Inc. is not affiliated with any educational institution.

We strongly recommend that students check with exam providers for up-to-date information regarding test content.

Published by

Complete Test Preparation Inc.
Victoria BC Canada
Visit us on the web at https://www.test-preparation.ca
Printed in the USA

ISBN-13: 9781772450460

Version 7.6 May 2019

About Complete Test Preparation Inc.

The Complete Test Preparation Team has been publishing high quality study materials since 2005. Over one million students visit our websites every year, and thousands of students, teachers and parents all over the world (over 100 countries) have purchased our teaching materials, curriculum, study guides and practice tests.

Complete Test Preparation is committed to providing students with the best study materials and practice tests available on the market. Members of our team combine years of teaching experience, with experienced writers and editors, all with advanced degrees.

Feedback

We welcome your feedback. Email us at feedback@test-preparation.ca with your comments and suggestions. We carefully review all suggestions and often incorporate reader suggestions into upcoming versions. As a Print on Demand Publisher, we update our products frequently.

https://www.facebook.com/CompleteTestPreparation/

https://www.youtube.com/user/MrTestPreparation

https://www.instagram.com/completetestpreparation/

https://www.pinterest.ca/brians6634/boards/

Contents

6   **Getting Started**
        How this study guide is organized   7
        Making a Study Schedule   7

13   **Practice Test Questions Set 1**
        Answer Key   63

81   **Practice Test Questions Set 2**
        Answer Key   126

140   **Conclusion**

Getting Started

CONGRATULATIONS! By deciding to take the Canadian Firefighter exam, you have taken the first step toward a great future! Of course, there is no point in taking this important examination unless you intend to do your best to earn the highest grade you possibly can. That means getting yourself organized and discovering the best approaches, methods and strategies to master the material. Yes, that will require real effort and dedication, but if you are willing to focus your energy and devote the study time necessary, before you know it you will be opening that letter of acceptance to the firefighter service of your choice!

We know that taking on a new endeavour can be scary, and it is easy to feel unsure of where to begin. That's where we come in. This study guide is designed to help you improve your test-taking skills, show you a few tricks of the trade and increase both your competency and confidence.

The Canadian Firefighter Test

The Canadian Firefighter exam is composed of five sections, reading comprehension, listening comprehension, basic math, mechanical aptitude and spatial perception.

While we seek to make our guide as comprehensive as possible, note that like all exams, the Canadian Firefighter Exam might be adjusted at some future point. New material might be added, or content that is no longer relevant or applicable might be removed. It is always a good idea to give the materials you receive when you register to take the exam a careful review.

How this study guide is organized

This study guide is divided into three sections. The first section, self-assessments, which will help you recognize your areas of strength and weaknesses. This will be a boon when it comes to managing your study time most efficiently; there is not much point of focusing on material you have already got firmly under control. Instead, taking the self-assessments will show you where that time could be much better spent. In this area you will begin with a few questions to evaluate quickly your understanding of material that is likely to appear on the Canadian Firefighter. If you do poorly in certain areas, simply work carefully through those sections in the tutorials and then try the self-assessment again.

The second section, Tutorials, offers information in each of the content areas, as well as strategies to help you master that material. The tutorials are not intended to be a complete course, but cover general principles. If you find that you do not understand the tutorials, it is recommended that you seek out additional instruction.

Third, we offer two sets of practice test questions, similar to those on the Canadian Firefighter Exam.

Making a Study Schedule

To make your study time most productive you will need to develop a study plan. The purpose of the plan is to organize all the bits of pieces of information in such a way that you will not feel overwhelmed. Rome was not built in a day, and learning everything you will need to know to pass the Canadian Firefighter is going to take time, too. Arranging the material you need to learn into manageable chunks is the best way to go. Each study session should make you feel as though you have reached your goal, and your goal is simply to learn what you planned to learn during that particular session. Try to organize the content in such a way that each study session builds on previous ones. That way, you will retain the information, be better able to access it, and review the previous bits and pieces at the same time.

Self-assessment

The Best Study Tip! The very best study tip is to start early! The longer you study regularly, the more you will retain and 'learn' the material. Studying for 1 hour per day for 20 days is far better than studying for 2 hours for 10 days.

What don't you know?

The first step is to assess your strengths and weaknesses. You may already have an idea of where your weaknesses are, or you can take our Self-assessment modules for each of the content areas.

Exam Component	Rate 1 to 5
Reading Comprehension	
Listening comprehension	
Reading Comprehension	
Mathematics	
Basic Math & Arithmetic	
Word problems	
Geometry	
Mechanical Comprehension	

Making a Study Schedule

The key to making a study plan is to divide the material you need to learn into manageable sized pieces and learn it, while at the same time reviewing the material that you already know.

Using the table above, any scores of 3 or below, you need to spend time learning, reviewing and practicing this subject area. A score of 4 means you need to review the material, but you don't have to spend time re-learning. A score of 5 and you are OK with just an occasional review before the exam.
A score of 0 or 1 means you really need to work on this should allocate the most time and the highest priority.
Some students prefer a 5-day plan and others a 10-day plan. It also depends on how much time until the exam.

Here is an example of a 5-day plan based on an example from the table above:

Mechanical Comprehension: 1- Study 1 hour everyday – review on last day

Listening Comprehension: 4 - Review every second day

Geometry: 2 - Study 1 hour first day – then ½ hour everyday

Word problems: 5 - Review for ½ hour every other day

Reading Comprehension: 5 - Review for ½ hour every other day

Using this example, reading comprehension and word problems are good and only need occasional review. Geometry is good and needs 'some' review. Listening comprehension needs a fair amount of work and Mechanical Comprehension is very weak and need the most time. Based on this, here is a sample study plan:

Day	Subject	Time
Monday		
Study	Mechanical Comp.	1 hour
Study	Geometry	1 hour
½ hour break		
Study	Listening Comp.	1 hour
Review	Reading Comp.	½ hour
Tuesday		
Study	Mechanical Comp.	1 hour
Study	Word Problems	½ hour
½ hour break		
Study	Geometry	½ hour
Review	Word Problems	½ hour
Review	Reading Comp.	½ hour
Wednesday		
Study	Mechanical Comp.	1 hour
Study	Word Problems	½ hour
½ hour break		
Study	Geometry	½ hour
Review	Reading Comp.	½ hour
Review	Listening Comp.	½ hour
Thursday		
Study	Mechanical Comp.	½ hour
Study	Word Problems	½ hour
Review	Geometry	½ hour
½ hour break		
Review	Reading Comp.	½ hour
Review	Word Problems	½ hour
Friday		
Review	Listening comprehension	½ hour
Review	Geometry	½ hour
½ hour break		
Review	Word Problems	½ hour
Review	Mechanical Comp.	½ hour

Using this example, adapt the study plan to your own schedule. This schedule assumes 2 ½ - 3 hours available to study everyday for a 5 day period.

First, write out what you need to study and how much. Next figure out how many days before the test. Note, do NOT study on the last day before the test. On the last day before the test, you won't learn anything and will probably only confuse yourself.

Make a table with the days before the test and the number of hours you have available to study each day. We suggest working with 1 hour and ½ hour time slots.

Start filling in the blanks, with the subjects you need to study the most, getting the most time, and the most regular time slots (i.e. everyday) and the subjects that you know getting the least time (e.g. ½ hour every other day, or every 3rd day).

Tips for making a schedule

Once you make a schedule, stick with it! Make your study sessions reasonable. If you make a study schedule and don't stick with it, you set yourself up for failure. Instead, schedule study sessions that are a bit shorter and set yourself up for success! Make sure your study sessions are do-able. Studying is hard work, but after you pass, you can party and take a break!

Schedule breaks. Breaks are just as important as study time. Work out a rotation of studying and breaks that works for you.

Build up study time. If you find it hard to sit still and study for 1 hour straight through, build up to it. Start with 20 minutes, and then take a break. Once you get used to 20-minute study sessions, increase the time to 30 minutes. Gradually work you way up to 1 hour.

How to Make a Study Plan and Schedule
https://www.test-preparation.ca/make-study-plan/

40 minutes to 1 hour is optimal. Studying for longer than this is tiring and not productive. Studying for shorter isn't long enough to be productive.

Studying Math. Studying Math is different from studying other subjects because you use a different part of your brain. The best way to study math is to practice everyday. This will train your mind to think in a mathematical way. If you miss a day or days, the mathematical mind-set is gone and you have to start all over again to build it up.

Study and practice math everyday for at least 5 days before the exam.

For more information, see our How to Study Guide at www.study-skills.ca.

Practice Test Questions Set 1

THE PRACTICE TEST PORTION PRESENTS QUESTIONS THAT ARE REPRESENTATIVE OF THE TYPE OF QUESTION YOU SHOULD EXPECT TO FIND ON THE CANADIAN FIREFIGHTER EXAM. **The questions here are for skill practice only.**

For the best results, take this Practice Test as if it were the real exam. Set aside time when you will not be disturbed, and a location that is quiet and free of distractions. Read the instructions carefully, read each question carefully, and answer to the best of your ability.

Use the bubble answer sheets provided. When you have completed the Practice Test, check your answer against the Answer Key and read the explanation provided.

Reading Comprehension Answer Sheet

	A	B	C	D	E		A	B	C	D	E
1	○	○	○	○	○	21	○	○	○	○	○
2	○	○	○	○	○	22	○	○	○	○	○
3	○	○	○	○	○	23	○	○	○	○	○
4	○	○	○	○	○	24	○	○	○	○	○
5	○	○	○	○	○	25	○	○	○	○	○
6	○	○	○	○	○	26	○	○	○	○	○
7	○	○	○	○	○	27	○	○	○	○	○
8	○	○	○	○	○	28	○	○	○	○	○
9	○	○	○	○	○	29	○	○	○	○	○
10	○	○	○	○	○	30	○	○	○	○	○
11	○	○	○	○	○						
12	○	○	○	○	○						
13	○	○	○	○	○						
14	○	○	○	○	○						
15	○	○	○	○	○						
16	○	○	○	○	○						
17	○	○	○	○	○						
18	○	○	○	○	○						
19	○	○	○	○	○						
20	○	○	○	○	○						

Listening Comprehension Answers Sheet

	A	B	C	D
1	○	○	○	○
2	○	○	○	○
3	○	○	○	○
4	○	○	○	○
5	○	○	○	○
6	○	○	○	○
7	○	○	○	○
8	○	○	○	○
9	○	○	○	○
10	○	○	○	○
11	○	○	○	○
12	○	○	○	○
13	○	○	○	○
14	○	○	○	○
15	○	○	○	○
16	○	○	○	○
17	○	○	○	○
18	○	○	○	○
19	○	○	○	○
20	○	○	○	○

Mathematics Answer Sheet

	A	B	C	D	E		A	B	C	D	E
1	○	○	○	○	○	21	○	○	○	○	○
2	○	○	○	○	○	22	○	○	○	○	○
3	○	○	○	○	○	23	○	○	○	○	○
4	○	○	○	○	○	24	○	○	○	○	○
5	○	○	○	○	○	25	○	○	○	○	○
6	○	○	○	○	○	26	○	○	○	○	○
7	○	○	○	○	○	27	○	○	○	○	○
8	○	○	○	○	○	28	○	○	○	○	○
9	○	○	○	○	○	29	○	○	○	○	○
10	○	○	○	○	○	30	○	○	○	○	○
11	○	○	○	○	○						
12	○	○	○	○	○						
13	○	○	○	○	○						
14	○	○	○	○	○						
15	○	○	○	○	○						
16	○	○	○	○	○						
17	○	○	○	○	○						
18	○	○	○	○	○						
19	○	○	○	○	○						
20	○	○	○	○	○						

Mechanical Aptitude Answer Sheet

	A	B	C	D	E			A	B	C	D	E
1	○	○	○	○	○		21	○	○	○	○	○
2	○	○	○	○	○		22	○	○	○	○	○
3	○	○	○	○	○		23	○	○	○	○	○
4	○	○	○	○	○		24	○	○	○	○	○
5	○	○	○	○	○		25	○	○	○	○	○
6	○	○	○	○	○		26	○	○	○	○	○
7	○	○	○	○	○		27	○	○	○	○	○
8	○	○	○	○	○		28	○	○	○	○	○
9	○	○	○	○	○		29	○	○	○	○	○
10	○	○	○	○	○		30	○	○	○	○	○
11	○	○	○	○	○							
12	○	○	○	○	○							
13	○	○	○	○	○							
14	○	○	○	○	○							
15	○	○	○	○	○							
16	○	○	○	○	○							
17	○	○	○	○	○							
18	○	○	○	○	○							
19	○	○	○	○	○							
20	○	○	○	○	○							

Reading Comprehension

Directions: The following questions are based on several reading passages. Each passage is followed by a series of questions. Read each passage carefully, and then answer the questions based on it. You may reread the passage as often as you wish. When you have finished answering the questions based on one passage, go right onto the next passage. Choose the best answer based on the information given and implied.

Questions 1 – 4 refer to the following passage.

Firefighters are on call 24 hours a day, 7 days a week, 365 days a year - even on Christmas day! They provide an essential service in all countries. A firefighter's job can be quite tedious on-call, and then very stressful when responding to an emergency. They are responsible for attaching hoses to hydrants, using powerful pumps, as well as "flying" up ladders, and using various tools to break through windows and doors. A firefighter's duties also include entering burning buildings to rescue victims. Some firefighters are trained for providing on-site medical attention. Research conducted by the National Fire Protection Association, suggests most calls firefighters respond to are medical emergencies, and not fires. Firefighters perform other rescue tasks such as rescuing animals from trees.

Firefighters have to be very well rounded and capable of conducting a variety of tasks at the scene of an emergency. Some firefighters require forensic skills to determine the cause of a fire. A firefighters' duties may vary a lot of times while at the scene of an emergency. In some instances, they have to remain at the scene of a disaster for weeks, freeing trapped victims and providing medical assistance.

While at the station, firefighters are on-call always. During this time, they inspect equipment, conduct drills to stay sharp, as well as eat and sleep during a 24 hour shift.

There are different types of fires hence the need or different types of firefighters. Some of the various types of fire fighters include forest, structural, aircraft and shipboard firefighters.

Forest firefighters, also called Wildland Firefighters, use a variety of heavy equipment along with water hoses to tame forest fires. They often create fire lines which control the fire by starving it of fuel. There is a special team of firefighters called smoke jumpers who parachute from airplanes to target hard to reach areas of forest fires.

1. Which paragraph best summarizes the job of firefighters?

    a. First paragraph

    b. Third paragraph

    c. Fourth paragraph

    d. Last paragraph

2. Under which category of firefighters would you place smoke jumpers?

    a. Structural

    b. Shipboard

    c. Forest

    d. Air craft

3. What is the aim of this passage?

    a. To show that fire fighters work throughout the year

    b. Outlines the work of fire fighters

    c. Highlight the different types of firefighters

    d. All of the above

4. Which of the following are firefighters mostly called to respond to?

    a. Rescue animals

    b. Putting out fires

    c. Medical emergencies

    d. Carrying out search and rescue

Questions 5 – 8 refer to the following passage.

Low Blood Sugar

As the name suggest, low blood sugar is low sugar levels in the bloodstream. This can occur when you have not eaten properly and undertake strenuous activity, or, when you are very hungry. When Low blood sugar occurs regularly and is ongoing, it is a medical condition called hypoglycemia. This condition can occur in diabetics and in healthy adults.

Causes of low blood sugar can include excessive alcohol consumption, metabolic problems, stomach surgery, pancreas, liver or kidneys problems, as well as a side-effect of some medications.

Symptoms

There are different symptoms depending on the severity of the case.

Mild hypoglycemia can lead to feelings of nausea and hunger. The patient may also feel nervous, jittery and have fast heart beats. Sweaty skin, clammy and cold skin are likely symptoms.

Moderate hypoglycemia can result in short temperedness, confusion, nervousness, fear and blurring of vision. The patient may feel weak and unsteady.

Severe cases of hypoglycemia can lead to seizures, coma, fainting spells, nightmares, headaches, excessive sweats and severe tiredness.

Diagnosis of low blood sugar

A doctor can diagnosis this medical condition by asking the patient questions and testing blood and urine samples. Home testing kits are available for patients to monitor blood sugar levels. It is important to see a qualified doctor though. The doctor can administer tests to ensure that will safely rule out other medical conditions that could affect blood sugar levels.

Treatment

Quick treatments include drinking or eating foods and drinks with high sugar contents. Good examples include soda, fruit juice, hard candy and raisins. Glucose energy tablets can also help. Doctors may also recommend medications and well as changes in diet and exercise routine to treat chronic low blood sugar.

5. Based on the article, which of the following is true?

    a. Low blood sugar can happen to anyone.

    b. Low blood sugar only happens to diabetics.

    c. Low blood sugar can occur even.

    d. None of the statements are true.

6. Which of the following are the author's opinion?

    a. Quick treatments include drinking or eating foods and drinks with high sugar contents.

    b. None of the statements are opinions.

    c. This condition can occur in diabetics and in healthy adults.

    d. There are different symptoms depending on the severity of the case

7. What is the author's purpose?

    a. To inform
    b. To persuade
    c. To entertain
    d. To analyze

8. Which of the following is not a detail?

    a. A doctor can diagnosis this medical condition by asking the patient questions and testing.
    b. A doctor will test blood and urine samples.
    c. Glucose energy tablets can also help.
    d. Home test kits monitor blood sugar levels.

Questions 9 - 12 refer to the following passage.

Passage 2 - When a Poet Longs to Mourn, He Writes an Elegy

Poems are an expressive, especially emotional, form of writing. They have been in literature virtually from the time civilizations invented the written word. Poets often portrayed as moody, secluded, and even troubled, but this is because poets are introspective and feel deeply about the current events and cultural norms they are surrounded with. Poets often produce the most telling literature, giving insight into the society and mind-set they come from. This can be done in many forms.

The oldest types of poems often include many stanzas, may or may not rhyme, and are more about telling a story than experimenting with language or words. The most common types of ancient poetry are epics, which are usually extremely long stories that follow a hero through his journey, or elegies, which are often solemn in tone and used to mourn or lament something or someone. The Mesopotamians are often said to have invented the written word, and their literature is among the oldest in the world, including the epic poem titled "Epic of Gilgamesh." Similar in style and length to "Gilgamesh" is "Beowulf," an elegy poem written in Old English and set in Scandinavia. These poems are often used by professors as the earliest examples of literature.

The importance of poetry was revived in the Renaissance. At this time, Europeans discovered the style and beauty of ancient Greek arts, and poetry was among those. Shakespeare is the most well-known poet of the time, and he used poetry not only to write poems but also to write plays for the theater. The most popular forms of poetry during the Renaissance included villanelles (a nineteen-line poem with two rhymes throughout), sonnets, as well as the epic. Poets during this time focused on style and form, and developed very specific rules and outlines for how an exceptional poem should be written.

As often happens in the arts, modern poets have rejected the constricting rules of Renaissance poets, and free form poems are much more popular. Some modern poems would read just like stories if they weren't arranged into lines and stanzas. It is difficult to tell which poems and poets will be the most important, because works of art often become more famous in hindsight, after the poet has died and society can look at itself without being in the moment. Modern poetry continues to develop, and will no doubt continue to change as values, thought, and writing continue to change.

Poems can be among the most enlightening and uplifting texts for a person to read if they are looking to connect with the past, connect with other people, or try to gain an understanding of what is happening in their time.

9. In summary, the author has written this passage

    a. as a foreword that will introduce a poem in a book or magazine

    b. because she loves poetry and wants more people to like it

    c. to give a brief history of poems

    d. to convince students to write poems

10. The author organizes the paragraphs mainly by

    a. moving chronologically, explaining which types of poetry were common in that time

    b. talking about new types of poems each paragraph and explaining them a little

    c. focusing on one poet or group of people and the poems they wrote

    d. explaining older types of poetry so she can talk about modern poetry

11. The author's claim that poetry has been around "virtually from the time civilizations invented the written word" is supported by the detail that

    a. Beowulf is written in Old English, which is not really in use any longer

    b. epic poems told stories about heroes

    c. the Renaissance poets tried to copy Greek poets

    d. the Mesopotamians are credited with both inventing the word and writing "Epic of Gilgamesh"

12. According to the passage, the word "telling" means

    a. speaking

    b. significant

    c. soothing

    d. wordy

Questions 13 – 15 refer to the following passage.

Passage 4 If You Have Allergies, You're Not Alone

People who experience allergies might joke that their immune systems have let them down or are seriously lacking. Truthfully though, people who experience allergic reactions or allergy symptoms during certain times of the year have heightened immune systems that are "better" than those of people who have perfectly healthy but less militant immune systems.

Still, when a person has an allergic reaction, they are having an adverse reaction to a substance that is considered normal to most people. Mild allergic reactions usually have symptoms like itching, runny nose, red eyes, or bumps or discoloration of the skin. More serious allergic reactions, such as those to animal and insect poisons or certain foods, may result in the closing of the throat, swelling of the eyes, low blood pressure, an inability to breath, and can even be fatal.

Different treatments help different allergies, and which one a person uses depends on the nature and severity of the allergy. It is recommended to patients with severe allergies to take extra precautions, such as carrying an EpiPen, which treats anaphylactic shock and may prevent death, always in order for the remedy to be readily available and more effective. When an allergy is not so severe, treatments may be used just relieve a person of uncomfortable symptoms. Over the counter allergy medicines treat milder symptoms, and can be bought at any grocery store and used in moderation to help people with allergies live normally.

There are many tests available to assess whether a person has allergies or what they may be allergic to, and advances in these tests and the medicine used to treat patients continues to improve. Despite this fact, allergies still affect many people throughout the year or even every day. Medicines used to treat allergies have side-effects, and it is difficult to bring the body into balance with the use of medicine. Regardless, many of those who live with allergies are grateful for what is available and find it useful in maintaining their lifestyles.

13. According to this passage, which group does the word "militant" belong in

    a. sickly, ailing, faint

    b. strength, power, vigor

    c. active, fighting, warring

    d. worn, tired, breaking down

14. The author says that "medicines used to treat allergies have side-effects" to

    a. point out that doctors aren't very good at diagnosing and treating allergies

    b. argue that because of the large number of people with allergies, a cure will never be found

    c. explain that allergy medicines aren't cures and some compromise must be made

    d. argue that more wholesome remedies should be researched and medicines banned

15. It can be inferred that _____ recommend that some people with allergies carry medicine with them.

    a. the author

    b. doctors

    c. the makers of EpiPen

    d. people with allergies

Questions 16 - 19 refer to the following passage.

Winged Victory of Samothrace: the Statue of the Gods

Students who read about the "Winged Victory of Samothrace" probably won't be able to picture what this statue looks like. However, almost anyone who knows a little about statues will recognize it when they see it: it is the statue of a winged woman who does not have arms or a head. Even the most famous pieces of art may be recognized by sight but not by name.

This iconic statue is of the Greek goddess Nike, who represented victory and was called Victoria by the Romans. The statue is sometimes called the "Nike of Samothrace." She was often displayed in Greek art as driving a chariot, and her speed or efficiency with the chariot may be what her wings symbolize. It is said that the statue was created around 200 BCE to celebrate a battle that was won at sea. Archaeologists and art historians believe the statue may have originally been part of a temple or other building, even one of the most important temples, Megaloi Theoi, just as many statues were used during that time.

"Winged Victory" does indeed appear to have had arms and a head when it was originally created, and it is unclear why they were removed or lost. Indeed, they have never been discovered, even with all the excavation that has taken place. Many speculate that one of her arms was raised and put to her mouth, as though she was shouting or calling out, which is consistent with the idea of her as a war figure. If the missing pieces were ever to be found, they might give Greek and art historians more of an idea of what Nike represented or how the statue was used. Learning about pieces of art through details like these can help students remember time frames or locations, as well as learn about the people who occupied them.

16. The author's title says the statue is "of the Gods" because

    a. the statue is very beautiful and even a god would find it beautiful

    b. the statue is of a Greek goddess, and gods were of primary importance to the Greek

    c. Nike lead the gods into war

    d. the statues were used at the temple of the gods and so it belonged to them

17. The third paragraph states that

    a. the statue is related to war and was probably broken apart by foreign soldiers

    b. the arms and head of the statue cannot be found because all the excavation has taken place

    c. speculations have been made about what the entire statue looked like and what it symbolized

    d. the statue has no arms or head because the sculptor lost them

18. The author's main purpose in writing this passage is to

    a. demonstrate that art and culture are related and one can teach us about the other

    b. persuade readers to become archaeologists and find the missing pieces of the statue

    c. teach readers about the Greek goddess Nike

    d. to teach readers the name of a statue they probably recognize

19. The author specifies the indirect audience as "students" because

   a. it is probably a student who is taking this test

   b. most young people don't know much about art yet and most young people are students

   c. students read more than people who are not students

   d. the passage is based on a discussion of what we can learn about culture from art

Questions 20 - 22 refer to the following passage.

Fires can be useful, deadly, destructive it all depends whether or not you can control it. There was a time when I thought that all fires could be extinguished with water, but boy was I wrong and I learned the hard way too. My father is an electrician and a pretty good one too, I remember he was working in the garage one day and just like that an electrical fire had started. I ran to get a bucket of water and swiftly threw it on the fire. Not only did the fire burn my father bet he also suffered electrical shocks. Little did I know that electrical fires can't be extinguished like that.

There are several different types of fires and they can't all be extinguished in the same way. While most fires can be extinguished using water, many require different means to be extinguished. Memory takes me back to a grade nine science class on combustion, when the teacher poured gasoline on the surface of water in a beaker, then lit it with a match. The fire walked on the surface of the water. I though this was impossible and even stated this in my hypothesis before the experiment. The teacher then covered the beaker with a piece of cardboard. I thought the fire would burn through the cardboard, but instead it went out. It was then explained that fire requires oxygen, fuel and heat to burn. When the oxygen is removed, the fire goes out.

There are many types of fire extinguishers on the market. Water and Foam extinguishers that snuffs out a fire by removing the heat from the fire; Carbon Dioxide fire extinguishers that put out fires by removing oxygen (fuel) from the fire. Dry Chemical fire extinguishers put out fires by disrupting the chemical reaction taking place in the fire. Dry Powder extinguishers work by separating the fuel from the oxygen or by removing heat from the fire.

Scientist are also constantly formulating new ways of putting out fires. Since 2015 a set of university students have discovered that even sound waves can extinguish fires.

20. What component of the fire did the teacher remove to extinguish the fire?

    a. Fuel

    b. Oxygen

    c. Heat

    d. All of the above

21. The purpose of the article is to

    a. Highlight ways of extinguishing fires

    b. Highlight the different types of fire extinguishers on the market

    c. Provide information on fires

    d. Distinguish between different types of fires

22. Which type of fire should NOT be extinguished by water?

    a. Forest fires

    b. Fires with gasoline as the fuel

    c. Electrical fires

    d. None of the above

Questions 23 – 26 refer to the following passage.

Ways Characters Communicate in Theater

Playwrights give their characters voices in a way that gives depth and added meaning to what happens on stage during their play. There are different types of speech in scripts that allow characters to talk with themselves, with other characters, and even with the audience.

It is very unique to theater that characters may talk "to themselves." When characters do this, the speech they give is called a soliloquy. Soliloquies are usually poetic, introspective, moving, and can tell audience members about the feelings, motivations, or suspicions of an individual character without that character having to reveal them to other characters on stage. "To be or not to be" is a famous soliloquy given by Hamlet as he considers difficult but important themes, such as life and death.

The most common type of communication in plays is when one character is speaking to another or a group of other characters. This is generally called dialogue, but can also be called monologue if one character speaks without being interrupted for a long time. It is not necessarily the most important type of communication, but it is the most common because the plot of the play cannot really progress without it.

Lastly, and most unique to theater (although it has been used somewhat in film) is when a character speaks directly to the audience. This is called an aside, and scripts usually specifically direct actors to do this. Asides are usually comical, an inside joke between the character and the audience, and very short. The actor will usually face the audience when delivering them, even if it's for a moment, so the audience can recognize this move as an aside.

All three of these types of communication are important to the art of theater, and have been perfected by famous playwrights like Shakespeare. Understanding these types of communication can help an audience member grasp what is artful about the script and action of a play.

23. According to the passage, characters in plays communicate to

   a. move the plot forward

   b. show the private thoughts and feelings of one character

   c. make the audience laugh

   d. add beauty and artistry to the play

24. When Hamlet delivers "To be or not to be," he can be described as

   a. solitary

   b. thoughtful

   c. dramatic

   d. hopeless

25. The author uses parentheses to punctuate "although it has been used somewhat in film"

   a. to show that films are less important

   b. instead of using commas so that the sentence is not interrupted

   c. because parenthesis help separate details that are not as important

   d. to show that films are not as artistic

26. What does the author mean by the phrase "give their characters voices?"

   a. playwrights are generous

   b. playwrights are changing the sound or meaning of characters' voices to fit what they had in mind

   c. dialogue is important in creating characters

   d. playwrights may be the parent of one of their actors and literally give them their voice

27. Consider the gauge above. What PSI is the limit of the safe working range?

    a. About 80 PSI
    b. About 90 PSI
    c. About 60 PSI
    d. About 100 PSI

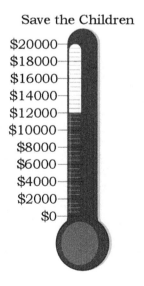

28. Consider the graphic above. The Save the Children fund has a fund-raising goal of $20,000. About how much of their goal have they achieved?

    a. 3/5
    b. 3/4
    c. 1/2
    d. 1/3

Questions 29 – 30 refer to the following passage.

The Life of a Firefighter

The life of a firefighter is pretty hectic, we are always on call, always training, always conducting drills and working 24 hours shift each day. "We practically live at work," as a colleague of mine puts it. Fires, like hurricanes are largely unpredictable, although they do have a season. The dry season always keeps us on our toes, and on some days we have to respond to simultaneous emergencies. On one particular day last week, putting out a fire in a warehouse was going smoothly, a hydrant was nearby, and the fire was almost under control. However, as we advanced into the building, we stumbled on an unconscious victim. I frenetically dashed towards the victim while my colleagues continued tackling the fire.

As firefighters, we are instinctively confident persons, however overconfidence can create complacency. I often make reference to the scenario mentioned above and pose the question: how would you respond? The unanimous response is usually, "get the victim and evacuate." This may sound plausible, however in the real world, it's not so simple; you may encounter another victim, or you can't go back the way you came, or you may get injured in the process. Therefore, grabbing an unconscious body and getting the person to safety is anything but simple.

During training sessions, the "casualties" are usually lifeless dummies that could never imitate the feel of an actual unconscious person, or the "casualties" are other colleagues who are usually very healthy. As firefighters, we must also be aware that environmental factors such as heat, smoke, and the lack of visibility may render some of the techniques we take for granted impractical or even harmful to the victim.

Most fires do not have casualties. This is due to upgrades in building construction, as well as easier and clearly marked exits to safely evacuate buildings. In addition, fire extinguishers are common and required by most building codes. As well, there is greater public awareness about fires and how to respond in an emergency has substantially reduced the number of casualties.

29. Why are fires compared to hurricanes?

   a. Both fires and hurricanes are devastating

   b. To show the destructive power of fires

   c. To show that fires are equally as powerful as hurricanes

   d. Both fires and hurricanes are unpredictable

30. According to the narrator, what may cause complacency among firefighters?

   a. Lack of confidence

   b. Overconfidence

   c. Overly preparedness

   d. Lack of training

Part II - Listening Comprehension

Directions: Scan the QR code below with any smartphone or tablet for an audio recording of the listening comprehension passages below. Or, have someone read them to you. Listen carefully to the passages and answer the questions that follow.

What is a QR Code?
A QR code looks like a barcode and it's used as a shortcut to link to content online using your phone's camera, saving you from typing lengthy addresses into your mobile browser.

Questions 8 – 11 refer to the following passage.

Fire Extinguishers

Fire extinguishers are used to put out or prevent small fires that are unexpected or accidental and has not reached the maximum burning potential and is controllable.

Fire extinguishers are placed in all buildings like companies, offices, government corporations and most people's homes. These extinguishers are serviced by a fire protection service company at least every year. Regular servicing is essential to prevent the unfortunate possibility they will be unavailable when really needed. Service companies provide services like, checking whether there is any replacement of the device needed as well as any recharging power.

Fire extinguishers can be handheld or cart-mounted, also called wheeled extinguisher. These two extinguishers have differences in weights. Handheld extinguishers weigh much less than cart-mounted extinguishers. Handheld generally weigh anywhere from 1 to 30 lbs., while cart-mounted extinguishers weigh more than 50 lbs. Wheel models are commonly found at construction sites, airport runways, heliports and docks.

Practice Test Questions 1

Scan for Audio or click
https://www.test-preparation.ca/audio/FireExtinguishers.wav

1. What types of fires are extinguishers NOT intended for?

    a. Electrical fires
    b. Out of control fires
    c. Fires on a boat or marina
    d. None of the above

2. How often are fire extinguishers inspected?

    a. Every 6 months
    b. There is no set time
    c. Every year
    d. Every 5 years

3. What are the two types of fire extinguishers?

    a. Stored pressure and cartridge-operated
    b. Chemical and water based
    c. Chemical and gas such as CO2
    d. None of the above

4. About how much do hand-held fire extinguishers weigh?

    a. 20 pounds
    b. 1 - 30 pounds
    c. 10 pounds
    d. 50 pounds

Questions 5 – 8 refer to the following passage.

Flame

Flames are the visible gaseous part of the fire. Flames have a wide range of colors and temperatures, which depends on the type of fuel. Fire continues to burn in a chain reaction that feeds on itself. The heat from the fire reaction vaporizes fuel molecules, which react with oxygen, creating more heat.

Incomplete combustion, generally of organic matter, produces an orange flame, releases less energy and produces carbon monoxide which is a poisonous gas.

When the combustion of a gas is complete the flame is blue.

The color of the flame, as well as the temperature, and therefore the rate of combustion depend on the fuel and oxygen supply mix.

Many combustion reactions do not require a flame, such as the reaction in an internal combustion engine. Various ways are used to eliminate a flame in combustion engines depending on the type of fuel.

Scan for audio or click
https://www.test-preparation.ca/audio/Flame-2.mp3

5. Under what conditions is a flame orange-red?

    a. Flames are always orange red

    b. Flames are orange red when burning non-organic matter

    c. Burning organic matter and the incomplete combustion of gas

    d. None of the above

6. When are flames blue?

    a. When the gases are not completely combusted

    b. When the gases are complete combusted

    c. When burning non-organic matter

    d. None of the above

7. Is oxygen always present for a flame to burn?

    a. Yes

    b. No

8. What color is the flame in combustion engines?

    a. Red

    b. Orange

    c. White

    d. There is no flame in combustion engines

Questions 9 – 11 refer to the following passage.

Fire

Fire has both positive and negative effects for humans as well as ecosystems. Fire is used for food preparations, providing heat for warmth, light, smoke is often a a sign of danger.

Forest fires have a major impact on ecosystems, restoring and rejuvenating by turning dead trees and decaying plant matters into ashes and returning nutrients into the soil. Atmospheric pollution from fire has a major negative effect on the environment. Air pollution from fire and combustion kills millions of people every year worldwide.

Scan for audio or click
https://www.test-preparation.ca/audio/Fire-3.mp3

9. What are some positive effects of fire?

    a. heat, light and smoke
    b. Returning dead trees to the soil
    c. Restoring nutrients to the soil
    d. None of the above

10. What are some positive effects of fire on the ecosystem?

    a. Rejuvenating the soil
    b. Providing heat and warmth
    c. Warning of danger
    c. None of the above

11. What is a major negative effect of fire?

    a. Signalling danger
    b. Returning dead trees to the soil
    c. Air Pollution
    d. None of the above

Questions 12 - 14 refer to the following passage.

Insects

Insects were the first animals able to fly. Most, but not all insects have wings, and all have six legs. Their life-cycle varies but most hatch eggs. Insects undergo a transformation process, called metamorphosis, where the immature insects undergo two or three stages. Insects outgrow their bodies and shed, or molt their old body several times.

Adult insects walk, sometimes swim, or fly.

Most insects have a walking style called tripedal. In this walking style or gait, their six legs touch the ground in alternating triangles. This gait allows for very rapid movement. Insects are mostly solitary but some, such as ants or bees live in colonies. Even though insect colonies have hundreds of individuals, they function together as one organism.

Insects are found all over the world, in virtually every environment. A few even live in the ocean. Some insects feed on fruit and crops and are classified as pests, and controlled with pesticides and other means. Others perform complex ecological roles and some spread disease.

Insects communicate in a variety of ways. For example, some insects, like crickets, produce a sound, by rubbing their legs together. Some beetles communicate with light.

Scan for audio or click
https://www.test-preparation.ca/audio/Insects-3.mp3

12. Choose the correct sentence.

    a. No insects can swim.

    b. All insects are excellent swimmers.

    c. Some insects are excellent swimmers.

    d. Most insects are excellent swimmers.

13. Choose the correct sentence.

    a. All insects communicate with sound.

    b. No insects communicate with sound.

    c. Insects don't communicate

    d. Many insects communicate with sound.

14. Are insects solitary or social?

    a. Solitary

    b. Social

    c. Some are social and some are solitary

    d. None of the above

Questions 15 - 16 refer to the following passage.

Trees

Trees are essential part of our natural ecosystem and provide shelter, fuel, medicine and much more. One of the principal benefits of trees is the photosynthesis process where carbon dioxide is absorbed, and oxygen released. Trees are also important in preventing erosion. Trees remove many types of pollutants in addition to carbon dioxide.

Trees have many practical applications. Wood is a fuel for heat as well as cooking for much of the world. Timber is used for construction, and pulp from wood is used to make paper.

Tree bark provides important medicines such as aspirin and quinine.

Practice Test Questions 1

Scan for audio or click
https://www.test-preparation.ca/audio/Trees-3.mp3

15. What are two reasons trees are important in the natural landscape?

    a. They prevent erosion and produce oxygen.

    b. They produce fruit and are important elements in c. landscaping.

    c. Trees are not important in the natural landscape.

    d. Trees produce carbon dioxide and prevent erosion.

16. What do trees do to the atmosphere?

    a. Trees produce carbon dioxide and reduce oxygen.

    b. Trees produce oxygen and carbon dioxide.

    c. Trees reduce oxygen and carbon dioxide.

    d. Trees produce oxygen and reduce carbon dioxide.

Questions 17 - 20 refer to the following passage.

Fire Fighters

Firefighters are trained to put out any type of fire and perform many types of rescues. There are fire departments in almost every country in the world. Firefighters are one of the three main emergency services, along with the police department and the emergency medical services.

Firefighters receive extensive training in firefighting to assure that they are prepared to handle any situation. While on duty, firemen or firewomen might have to deal with fire prevention, fire suppression, ventilation, containment, search and rescue, and many other situations.

The main goal of the fire departments is to save lives, protect property, and protect the environment from the dangers of fires. Traditionally, the firefighters are associated with Dalmatians as helper animals. While most fire departments use dogs, they are not Dalmatians. Fire departments only used dogs for rescue operations, and keep them away from fires.

Scan for Audio or click
https://www.test-preparation.ca/audio/Firefighters.mp3

17. What are the three main emergency services?

    a. Fire departments, emergency medical and police

    b. Fire departments, emergency medical and highway patrol

    c. RCMP, fire departments and emergency medical

    d. Disaster relief, fire departments, and emergency medical

8. What are the main goals of the fire department?

  a. Put out fires and protect property

  b. To save lives, protect property and protect the environment

  c. To save lives, put out fires and protect property

  d. To protect property, save the environment and put out fires

19. What animal is traditionally associated with firefighters?

  a. Dogs

  b. Dalmatians

  c. Horses

  d. No animal

20. Do animals assist firefighters putting out fires?

  a. Yes

  b. No

  c. The articles doesn't say.

Part III - Mathematics

1. What is 1/3 of 3/4?

  a. 1/4

  b. 1/3

  c. 2/3

  d. 3/4

2. What fraction of $1500 is $75?

   a. 1/14
   b. 3/5
   c. 7/10
   d. 1/20

3. 3.14 + 2.73 + 23.7 =

   a. 28.57
   b. 30.57
   c. 29.56
   d. 29.57

4. A woman spent 15% of her income on an item and ends with $120. What percentage of her income is left?

   a. 12%
   b. 85%
   c. 75%
   d. 95%

5. Express 0.27 + 0.33 as a fraction.

   a. 3/6
   b. 4/7
   c. 3/5
   d. 2/7

6. What is (3.13 + 7.87) X 5?

   a. 65
   b. 50
   c. 45
   d. 55

Practice Test Questions 1 47

7. Reduce 2/4 X 3/4 to lowest terms.

    a. 6/12
    b. 3/8
    c. 6/16
    d. 3/4

8. 2/3 − 2/5 =

    a. 4/10
    b. 1/15
    c. 3/7
    d. 4/15

9. 2/7 + 2/3 =

    a. 12/23
    b. 5/10
    c. 20/21
    d. 6/21

10. 2/3 of 60 + 1/5 of 75 =

    a. 45
    b. 55
    c. 15
    d. 50

11. 8 is what percent of 40?

    a. 10%
    b. 15%
    c. 20%
    d. 25%

12. 9 is what percent of 36?

   a. 10%
   b. 15%
   c. 20%
   d. 25%

13. Three tenths of 90 equals:

   a. 18
   b. 45
   c. 27
   d. 36

14. .4% of 36 is

   a. .144
   b. 1.44
   c. 14.4
   d. 144

15. Convert 0.007 kilograms to grams

   a. 7 grams
   b. 70 grams
   c. 0.07 grams
   d. 0.70 grams

16. Convert 16 quarts to gallons

   a. 1 gallons
   b. 8 gallons
   c. 4 gallons
   d. 4.5 gallons

17. Convert 200 meters to kilometers

    a. 50 kilometers
    b. 20 kilometers
    c. 12 kilometers
    d. 0.2 kilometers

18. Convert 72 inches to feet

    a. 12 feet
    b. 6 feet
    c. 4 feet
    d. 17 feet

19. Convert 3 yards to feet

    a. 18 feet
    b. 12 feet
    c. 9 feet
    d. 27 feet

20. Convert 45 kg. to pounds.

    a. 10 pounds
    b. 100 pounds
    c. 1,000 pounds
    d. 110 pounds

21. Convert 0.63 grams to mg.

    a. 630 g.
    b. 63 mg.
    c. 630 mg.
    d. 603 mg.

22. The price of a book went up from $20 to $25. What percent did the price increase?

    a. 5%
    b. 10%
    c. 20%
    d. 25%

23. The price of a book decreased from $25 to $20. What percent did the price decrease?

    a. 5%
    b. 10%
    c. 20%
    d. 25%

24. After taking several practice tests, Brian improved the results of his GRE test by 30%. Given that the first time he took the test, he answered 150 questions correctly, how many questions did he answer correctly the second time?

    a. 105
    b. 120
    c. 180
    d. 195

25. On a local baseball team, 4 players (or 12.5% of the team) have long hair and the rest have short hair. How many short-haired players are there on the team?

    a. 24
    b. 28
    c. 32
    d. 50

Practice Test Questions 1   51

26. In the time required to serve 43 customers, a server breaks 2 glasses and slips 5 times. The next day, the same server breaks 10 glasses. Assuming the number of glasses broken is proportional to the number of customers, how many customers did she serve?

   a. 25
   b. 43
   c. 86
   d. 215

27. A square lawn has an area of 62,500 square meters. What will the cost of building fence around it at a rate of $5.5 per meter?

   a. $4000
   b. $4500
   c. $5000
   d. $5500

28. Mr. Brown bought 5 cheese burgers, 3 drinks, and 4 fries for his family, and a cookie pack for his dog. If the price of all single items is the same at $1.30 and a 3.5% tax is added, what is the total cost of dinner for Mr. Brown?

   a. $16
   b. $16.9
   c. $17
   d. $17.5

29. A distributor purchased 550 kilograms of potatoes for $165. He distributed these at a rate of $6.4 per 20 kilograms to 15 shops, $3.4 per 10 kilograms to 12 shops and the remainder at $1.8 per 5 kilograms. If his total distribution cost is $10, what will his profit be?

    a. $10.40
    b. $8.60
    c. $14.90
    d. $23.40

30. How much pay does Mr. Johnson receive if he gives half of his pay to his family, $250 to his landlord, and has exactly 3/7 of his pay left over?

    a. $3600
    b. $3500
    c. $2800
    d. $1750

Mechanical Comprehension

1. What is mechanical advantage?

    a. The ratio of energy input to energy output, typically where the input is less than the output.

    b. The ratio of energy input to energy output, typically where the input is greater than the output.

    c. The ratio of energy resistance to energy output, typically where the resistance is less than the output.

    d. None of the above

2. What is the ratio of mechanical advantage of a simple pulley?

    a. 2:1

    b. 1:1

    c. 3:1

    d. 1:2

3. Consider moving an object with a lever and a fulcrum. What is the relationship between the distance from the fulcrum and the speed the object will move?

    a. The farther away from the fulcrum, the faster the object will move.

    b. The closer to the fulcrum, the faster an object will move.

    c. An object will move the fastest when directly above the fulcrum.

    d. None of the above.

4. Which of the following are examples of a wedge?

    a. Corkscrew

    b. Scissors

    c. Wheelbarrow

    d. Pulley

5. Which of the following illustrates the principle of the lever?

    a. The greater the distance over which the force is applied, the greater the force required (to lift the load).

    b. The greater the distance over which the force is applied, the smaller the force required (to lift the load).

    c. The smaller the distance over which the force is applied, the smaller the force required (to lift the load).

    d. None of the above

6. Consider two gears on separate shafts that mesh. The input gear has 30 teeth and turns at 100 rpm. If the output gear has 40 teeth, how fast is the output gear turning?

    a. 300 rpm
    b. 250 rpm
    c. 75 rpm
    d. 100 rpm

7. Consider two gears on separate shafts that mesh. The input gear has 100 teeth and turns at 50 rpm. If the output gear has 20 teeth, how fast is the output gear turning?

    a. 300 rpm
    b. 250 rpm
    c. 200 rpm
    d. 100 rpm

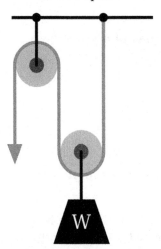

8. Consider the pulley arrangement above. If the weight is 100 pounds, how much force is required to lift it?

    a. 20 pounds
    b. 33 pounds

c. 50 pounds
d. 75 pounds

9. What type of screwdriver is used with the screw pictured above?

    a. Robertson
    b. Slot
    c. Philips
    d. Hex

10. Consider the pulley arrangement above. If the weight is 200 pounds, how much force must be exerted downward on the rope?

    a. 200 pounds
    b. 100 pounds
    c. 50 pounds
    d. 25 pounds

11. Up-and-down or back-and-forth motion is called:

   a. Rotary motion
   b. Reciprocating motion
   c. Agitation motion
   d. Harmonic motion

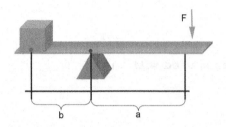

12. Consider the illustration above and the corresponding data:

Weight = W = 80 pounds
Distance from fulcrum to Weight = b = 10 feet
Distance from fulcrum to point where force is applied = a = 20 feet
How much force (F) must be applied to lift the weight?

   a. 80
   b. 40
   c. 20
   d. 10

13. Which of the following is an example of torque?

   a. The wheel of a pulley turning
   b. A piston moving
   c. A horse pulling a load
   d. A tow truck pulling a vehicle

14. Which of the following floor plans match the house shown below?

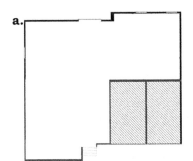

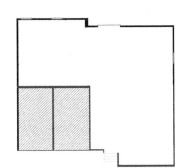

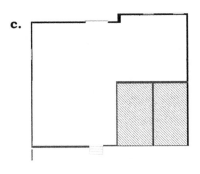

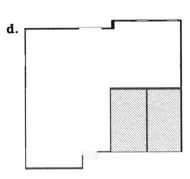

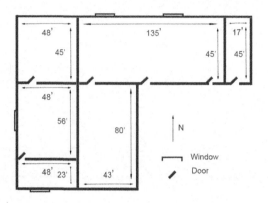

Note: figure not drawn to scale

15. What is the north south width of the house above?

    a. 124
    b. 100
    c. 200
    d. 224

16. What is the east west length of the house above?

    a. 200
    b. 124
    c. 100
    d. 224

17. Which of the following floor plans match the house shown below?

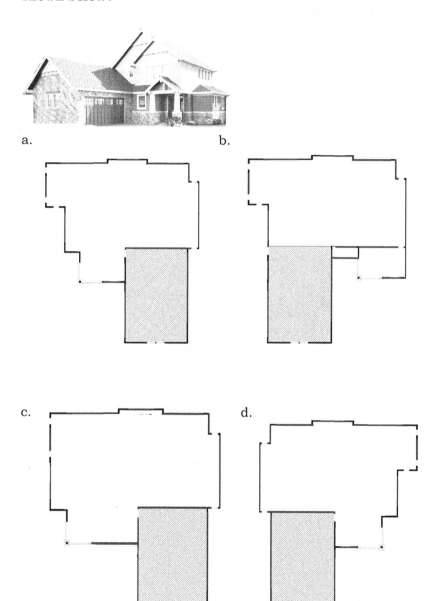

18.

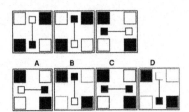

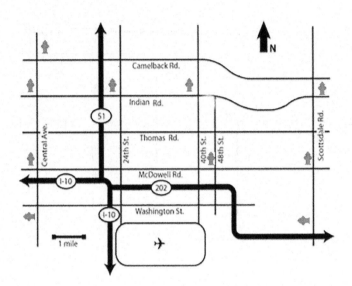

19. Consider the map above. How many hydrants are on Indian Road?

    a. 1
    b. 2
    c. 3
    d. 4

20. What is the best route from the east exit of the airport to the corner of Camelback and Central?

a. Exit the airport onto 40th st. and proceed north, turn left on Camelback Rd. and proceed straight to the corner of Central Ave.

b. Exit the airport on 24th st. and proceed north, turn left on Camelback Rd. and proceed straight to the corner of Central Ave.

c. Exit the airport onto 40th st. and turn west on hwy 202, then north on hwy 1-10, then right on hwy 51 then exit on Camelback Rd. and proceed strait to the corner of central.

d. None of the above.

21. About how far is the corner of Scottsdale Rd. and Thomas Rd. to the corder of Central Ave. and Thomas Rd.?

a. 4 miles
b. 3 miles
c. 5 miles
d. 7 miles

22.

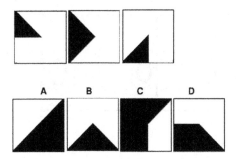

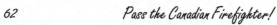

23.

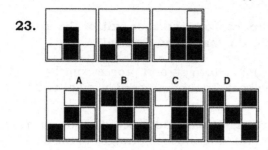

24. When the two longest sides touch, what will the shape be?

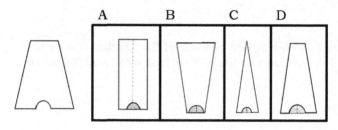

25. When folded, what pattern is possible?

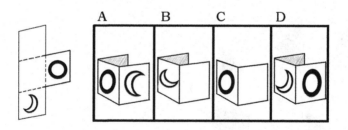

Answer Key

Part 1 – Reading Comprehension

1. A
The first paragraph provides a summary of firefighter's job. The second paragraph is mainly about different tasks a firefighter performs. The third paragraph is about being on-call. The fourth paragraph is about different types of fires. And the last paragraph is about forest firefighters.

2. C
Smoke jumpers are forest firefighters. The last paragraph highlights this fact.

3. D
All of the above. Choices A, B and C are all aims of the passage hence choice D is the correct response.

   a. to show that fire fighters work throughout the year
   b. outlines the work of fire fighters
   c. highlight the different types of firefighters

4. C
Firefighters most frequently respond to medical emergencies. This is clearly highlighted in the first paragraph.

5. A
Low blood sugar occurs both in diabetics and healthy adults.

6. B
None of the statements are the author's opinion.

7. A
The author's purpose is to inform.

8. A
The only statement that is **not** a detail is, "A doctor can diag-

nosis this medical condition by asking the patient questions and testing."

9. C
This question tests the reader's summarization skills. The use of the word "actually" in describing what kind of people poets are, as well as other moments like this, may lead readers to selecting choice B or D, but the author is more information than trying to persuade readers. The author gives no indication that she loves poetry (B) or that people, students specifically (D), should write poems. Choice A is incorrect because the style and content of this paragraph do not match those of a foreword; forewords usually focus on the history or ideas of a specific poem to introduce it more fully and help it stand out against other poems. The author here focuses on several poems and gives broad statements. Instead, she tells a kind of story about poems, giving three very broad time periods in which to discuss them, thereby giving a brief history of poetry, as choice C states.

10. A
This question tests the reader's summarization skills. Key words in the topic sentences of each of the paragraphs ("oldest," "Renaissance," "modern") should give the reader an idea that the author is moving chronologically. The opening and closing sentence-paragraphs are broad and talk generally. Choice B seems reasonable, but epic poems are mentioned in two paragraphs, eliminating the idea that only new types of poems are used in each paragraph. Choice C is also easily eliminated because the author clearly mentions several different poets, groups of people, and poems. Choice D also seems reasonable, considering that the author does move from older forms of poetry to newer forms, but use of "so (that)" makes this statement false, for the author gives no indication that she is rushing (the paragraphs are about the same size) or that she prefers modern poetry.

11. D
This question tests the reader's attention to detail. The key word is "invented"--it ties together the Mesopotamians, who invented the written word, and the fact that they, as the inventors, also invented and used poetry. The other selections focus on other details mentioned in the passage, such as

that the Renaissance's admiration of the Greeks (C) and that Beowulf is in Old English (A). Choice B may seem like an attractive answer because it is unlike the others and because the idea of heroes seems rooted in ancient and early civilizations.

12. B
This question tests the reader's vocabulary and contextualization skills. "Telling" is not an unusual word, but it may be used here in a way that is not familiar to readers, as an adjective rather than a verb in gerund form. Choice A may seem like the obvious answer to a reader looking for a verb to match the use they are familiar with. If the reader understands that the word is being used as an adjective and that choice A is a ploy, they may opt to select choice D, "wordy," but it does not make sense in context. Choice C can be easily eliminated, and doesn't have any connection to the paragraph or passage. "Significant" (B) does make sense contextually, especially relative to the phrase "give insight" used later in the sentence.

13. C
This question tests the reader's vocabulary skills. The uses of the negatives "but" and "less," especially right next to each other, may confuse readers into answering with choices A or D, which list words that are the opposite of "militant." Readers may also be confused by the comparison of healthy people with what is being described as an overly healthy person -- both people are good, but the reader may look for which one is "worse" in the comparison, and therefore stray toward the opposite words.

One key to understanding the meaning of "militant" is to look at the root; and then easily associate it with "military" and gain a sense of what the word signifies: defense (especially considered that the immune system defends the body). Choice C is correct over B because "militant" is an adjective, just as the words in C are, whereas the words in choice B are nouns.

14. C
This question tests the reader's understanding of function within writing. The other choices are all details included surrounding the quoted text, and may therefore confuse the reader. Choice A somewhat contradicts what is said earlier in the paragraph, which is that tests and treatments are improving, and probably doctors are along with them, but the paragraph doesn't actually mention doctors, and the subject of the question is the medicine. Choice B may seem correct to readers who aren't careful to understand that, while the author does mention the large number of people affected, the author is touching on the realities of living with allergies, rather than the likelihood of curing all allergies. Similarly, while the the author does mention the "balance" of the body, which is easily associated with "wholesome," the author is not really making an argument and especially is not making an extreme statement that allergy medicines should be outlawed. Again, because the article's tone is on living with allergies, choice C is an appropriate choice that fits with the title and content of the text.

15. B
This question tests the reader's inference skills. The text does not state who is doing the recommending, but the use of the "patients," as well as the general context of the passage, lends itself to the logical partner, "doctors," choice B.

The author does mention the recommendation but doesn't present it as her own (i.e. "I recommend that"), so choice A may be eliminated. It may seem plausible that people with allergies (choice D) may recommend medicines or products to other people with allergies, but the text does not necessarily support this interaction taking place. Choice C may be selected because the EpiPen is specifically mentioned, but the use of the phrase "such as" when it is introduced is not limiting enough to assume the recommendation is coming from its creators.

16. B
This question tests the reader's summarization skills. Choice A is a very broad statement that may or may not be true, and seems to be in context, but has nothing to do with the passage. The author does mention that the statue was prob-

ably used on a temple dedicated to the Greek gods (D), but in no way discusses or argues for the gods' attitude toward or claim on these temples or its faucets. Nike does indeed lead the gods into a war (the Titan war), as choice C suggests, but this is not mentioned by the passage and students who know this may be drawn to this answer but have not done a close enough analysis of the text that is actually in the passage. Choice B is appropriately expository, and connects the titular emphasis to the idea that the Greek gods are very important to Greek culture.

17. C
This question tests the reader's summarization skills. The test for question choice C is pulled straight from the paragraph, but is not word-for-word, so it may seem too obvious to be the right answer. The passage does talk about Nike being the goddess of war, as choice A states, but the third paragraph only touches on it and it is an inference that soldiers destroyed the statue, when this question is asking specifically for what the third paragraph actually stated. Choice B is also straight from the text, with a minor but key change: the inclusion of the words "all" and "never" are too limiting and the passage does not suggest that these limits exist. If a reader selects choice D, they are also making an inference that is misguided for this type of question. The paragraph does state that the arms and head are "lost" but does not suggest who lost them.

18. A
This question tests the reader's ability to recognize function in writing. Choice B can be eliminated based on the purpose of the passage, which is expository and not persuasive. The author may or may not feel this way, but the passage does not show evidence of being argumentative for that purpose. Choices C and D are both details found in the text, but neither of them encompasses the entire message of the passage, which has an overall message of learning about culture from art and making guesses about how the two are related, as suggested by choice A.

19. D
This question tests the reader's ability to understand function within writing. Most of the possible selections are very

general statements which may or may not be true. It probably is a student who is taking the test on which this question is featured (A), but the author makes no address to the test taker and is not talking to the audience in terms of the test. Likewise, it may also be true that students read more than adults (C), mandated by schools and grades, but the focus on the verb "read" in the first sentence is too narrow and misses the larger purpose of the passage; the same could be said for selection B. While all the statements could be true, choice D is the most germane, and infers the purpose of the passage without making assumptions that could be incorrect.

20. A
The purpose of the article is to highlight ways of extinguishing fires. This is the main theme of the passage and each paragraph speaks to a means of putting out fires.

21. C
The purpose is to provide information about fires.

22. C
Electrical fires cannot be extinguished by water. This can be inferred from the writers experience when he attempted to extinguish the fire in the garage.

23. D
This question tests the reader's summarization skills. The question is asking very generally about the message of the passage, and the title, "Ways Characters Communicate in Theater," is one indication of that. The other choices A, B, and C are all directly from the text, and therefore readers may be inclined to select one of them, but are too specific to encapsulate the entirety of the passage and its message.

24. B
The paragraph on soliloquies mentions "To be or not to be," and it is from the context of that paragraph that readers may understand that because "To be or not to be" is a soliloquy, Hamlet will be introspective, or thoughtful, while delivering it. It is true that actors deliver soliloquies alone, and may be "solitary" (A), but "thoughtful" (B) is more true

to the overall idea of the paragraph. Readers may choose C because drama and theater can be used interchangeably and the passage mentions that soliloquies are unique to theater (and therefore drama), but this answer is not specific enough to the paragraph in question. Readers may pick up on the theme of life and death and Hamlet's true intentions and select that he is "hopeless" (D), but those themes are not discussed either by this paragraph or passage, as a close textual reading and analysis confirms.

25. C
This question tests the reader's grammatical skills. Choice B seems logical, but parenthesis are actually considered to be a stronger break in a sentence than commas are, and along this line of thinking, actually disrupt the sentence more. Choices A and D make comparisons between theater and film that are simply not made in the passage, and may or may not be true. This detail does clarify the statement that asides are most unique to theater by adding that it is not completely unique to theater, which may have been why the author didn't chose not to delete it and instead used parentheses to designate the detail's importance (C).

26. C
This question tests the reader's vocabulary and contextualization skills. Choice A may or may not be true, but focuses on the wrong function of the word "give" and ignores the rest of the sentence, which is more relevant to what the passage is discussing. CHoices B and D may also be selected if the reader depends too literally on the word "give," failing to grasp the more abstract function of the word that is the focus of choice C, which also properly acknowledges the entirety of the passage and its meaning.

27. A
According to the gauge, the limit of the safe working range is about 80 PSI.

28. A
The Save the Children's fund has raised $12,000 out of $20,000, or 12/20. Simplifying, 12/20 = 3/5

29. D
Fires are compared to hurricanes as they are both unpredictable. This is clearly stated in the first paragraph.

30. B
Overconfidence can cause complacency. Choices A and C may seem plausible if you are in a hurry and don't check the passage carefully.

Part II - Listening Comprehension

1. B
Fire extinguishers are typically used for small fires and not intended for out-of-control fires, such as one which has reached the ceiling, or endangers the user.

2. C
Fire extinguishers are typically inspected every year, although some jurisdictions require more frequent inspections.

3. A
The two most common types of fire extinguishers are stored pressure and cartridge-operated.

4. A
Hand-held fire extinguishers weigh between 1 and 30 pounds.

5. C
The burning of organic matter like wood, or the incomplete combustion of gas, incandescent solid particles called soot produce the familiar red-orange glow of 'fire.'

6. B
Complete combustion of gas has a dim blue color.

7. A
Usually oxygen is necessary for a fire to burn.

8. D
There is no flame in combustion engines.

Practice Test Questions 1

9. C
One of the positive effects of fire is returning nutrients tok the soil.

10. A
A positive effect on the eco-system is rejuvenating the soil.

11. C
A negative effect of fire is air pollution.

12. C
From the passage, "some adult insects live underwater and are excellent swimmers."

13. D
From the passage, "Many insects communicate with sound."

14. C
Insects are mostly solitary, but some are social like ants and bees.

15. A
Choice A is a re-wording of text from the passage.

16. D
This question is designed to confuse by presenting different options for the 2 chemicals, oxygen and carbon dioxide. One is produced and one is reduced.

17. A
The three main emergency services are fire departments, emergency medical and police.

18. B
The three goals of the fire department are to save lives, protect property and protect the environment.

19. B
Dalmatians are traditionally associated with fire fighters.

20. B
From the Passage, "Fire departments only used dogs for res-

cue operations, and keep them away from fires. "

Part III - Mathematics

1. A
1/3 X 3/4 = 3/12 = 1/4

2. D
75/1500 = 15/300 = 3/60 = 1/20

3. D
3.14 + 2.73 = 5.87 and 5.87 + 23.7 = 29.57

4. B
Spent 15% - 100% - 15% = 85%

5. C
To convert a decimal to a fraction, take the places of decimal as your denominator, here 2, so in 0.27, '7' is in the 100th place, so the fraction is 27/100 and 0.33 becomes 33/100.

Next estimate the answer quickly to eliminate obvious wrong choices. 27/100 is about 1/4 and 33/100 is 1/3. 1/3 is slightly larger than 1/4, and 1/4 + 1/4 is 1/2, so the answer will be slightly larger than 1/2.

Looking at the choices, Choice A can be eliminated since 3/6 = 1/2. Choice D, 2/7 is less than 1/2 and can be eliminated. So the answer is going to be Choice B or Choice C.

Do the calculation, 0.27 + 0.33 = 0.60 and 0.60 = 60/100 = 3/5, Choice C is correct.

6. D
3.13 + 7.87 = 11 and 11 X 5 = 55

7. B
2/4 X 3/4 = 6/16, and reduced to the lowest terms = 3/8

8. D
2/3-2/5 = 10-6 /15 = 4/15

9. C
2/7 + 2/3 = 6+14 /21 (21 is the common denominator) = 20/21

10. B
2/3 x 60 = 40 and 1.5 x 75 = 15, 40 + 15 = 55

11. C
This is an easy question, and shows how you can solve some questions without doing the calculations. The question is, 8 is what percent of 40. Take easy percentages for an approximate answer and see what you get.

10% is easy to calculate because you can drop the zero, or move the decimal point. 10% of 40 = 4, and 8 = 2 X 4, so, 8 must be 2 X 10% = 20%.

Here are the calculations which confirm the quick approximation.
8/40 = X/100 = 8 * 100 / 40X = 800/40 = X = 20

12. D
This is the same type of question which illustrates another method to solve quickly without doing the calculations. The question is, 9 is what percent of 36?

Ask, what is the relationship between 9 and 36? 9 X 4 = 36 so they are related by a factor of 4. If 9 is related to 36 by a factor of 4, then what is related to 100 (to get a percent) by a factor of 4?

To visualize:

9 X 4 = 36
Z X 4 = 100

So the answer is 25. 9 has the same relation to 36 as 25 has to 100.
Here are the calculations which confirm the quick approximation.
9/36 = X/100 = 9 * 100 / 36X = 900/36 = 25

13. C
3/10 * 90 = 3 * 90/10 = 27

14. A
.4/100 * 36 = .4 * 36/100 = .144

15. A
1000g = 1kg., 0.007 = 1000 x 0.007 = 7g.

16. C
4 quarts = 1 gallon, 16 quarts = 16/4 = 4 gallons

17. D
1,000 meters = 1 kilometer, 200 m = 200/1,000 = 0.2 km.

18. B
12 inches = 1 ft., 72 inches = 72/12 = 6 feet

19. C
1 yard = 3 feet, 3 yards = 3 feet x 3 = 9 feet

20. B
0.45 kg = 1 pound, 1 kg. = 1/0.45 and 45 kg = 1/0.45 x 45 = 99.208, or 100 pounds

21. C
1 g = 1,000 mg. 0.63 g = 0.63 x 1,000 = 630 mg.

22. D
The price increased by $5 ($25-$20). The percent increase is 5/20 x 100 = 5 x 5=25%

23. C
The price decreased by $5 ($25-$20). The percent increase = 5/25 x 100 = 5 x 4 =20%

24. D
30/100 x 150 = 3 x 15 = 45 (increase in number of correct answers). So the number of correct answers on the second test = 150 + 45 = 195

25. B
Let total number of players= X

Let the number of players with long hair = Y and the number of players with short hair = Z
Then X = 4 + Z
Y = 12% of X
Z = X - 4
12.5% of X = 4
Converting from decimal to fraction gives 12.5% = 125/10 x 1/100 = 125/1000, therefore 12.5% of = 125/1000X = 4
Solve for X by multiplying both sides by 1000/125, X = 4 x 1000/125 = 32
Z = x – 4
Z = 32 – 4
z or number of short haired players = 28

26. D
2 glasses are broken for 43 customers so 1 glass breaks for every 43/2 customers served, therefore 10 glasses implies 43/2 x 10 = 215

27. D
As the lawn is square, the length of one side will be the square root of the area. √62,500 = 250 meters. So, the perimeter is 4 times the length of one side:

250 * 4 = 1000 meters.

Since each meter costs $5.5, the total cost of the fence will be 1000 * 5.5 = $5,500.

28. D
The price of all the single items is same and there are 13 total items. So the total cost will be 13 × 1.3 = $16.9. After 3.5 percent tax this amount will become 16.9 × 1.035 = $17.5.

29. B
The distribution is at three different rates and amounts:

$6.4 per 20 kilograms to 15 shops ... 20 * 15 = 300 kilograms distributed

$3.4 per 10 kilograms to 12 shops ... 10 * 12 = 120 kilograms distributed

550 - (300 + 120) = 550 - 420 = 130 kilograms left. This amount is distributed by 5 kilogram portions. So, this means that there are 130/5 = 26 shops.

$1.8 per 130 kilograms.

We need to find the amount he earned overall these distributions.

$6.4 per 20 kilograms : 6.4 * 15 = $96 for 300 kilograms

$3.4 per 10 kilograms : 3.4 * 12 = $40.8 for 120 kilograms

$1.8 per 5 kilograms : 1.8 * 26 = $46.8 for 130 kilograms

So, he earned 96 + 40.8 + 46.8 = $ 183.6

The total cost of distribution is given as $10

The profit is found by: Money earned - money spent ... It is important to remember that he bought 550 kilograms of potatoes for $165 at the beginning:

Profit = 183.6 - 10 - 165 = $8.6

30. B

We check the fractions in the question. We see that there is a "half" (that is 1/2) and 3/7. So, we multiply the denominators of these fractions to decide how to name the total money. We say that Mr. Johnson has 14x at the beginning; he gives half of this, meaning 7x, to his family. $250 to his landlord. He has 3/7 of his money left. 3/7 of 14x is equal to:

14x * (3/7) = 6x

So,

Spent money is: 7x + 250

Unspent money is: 6x

Total money is: 14x

We write an equation: total money = spent money + unspent money

14x = 7x + 250 + 6x

14x - 7x - 6x = 250

x = 250

We are asked to find the total money that is 14x:

14x = 14 * 250 = $3500

Part IV - Mechanical Aptitude

1. A
Mechanical advantage is the ratio of energy input to energy output, typically where the input is less than the output. Mechanical advantage is a measure of the force amplification achieved by using a tool, mechanical device or machine system. Ideally, the device preserves the input power and simply trades off forces against movement to obtain a desired amplification in the output force. The model for this is the law of the lever. Machine components designed to manage forces and movement in this way are called mechanisms. [11]

2. B
The ratio of mechanical advantage of a simple pulley is 1:1.

3. A
The farther away from the fulcrum, the faster the object will move.

4. B
Examples of wedges include the cutting edge of scissors, knives, screwdrivers, doorstops, nails axes and chisels.

5. B
The greater the distance over which the force is applied, the smaller the force required (to lift the load).

6. C
Call the input gear G_1 and the output gear G_2. Call the speed of G_1, S_1 and the number of teeth T_1. Similarly for G_2, we have S_2 and T_2.

Given data:
$S_1 = 100$
$T_1 = 30$

S_2 = unknown
T_2 = 40

We know that $S_1 \times T_1 = S_2 \times T_2$
So, $100 \times 30 = S_2 \times 40$
$S_2 = 3000/40 = 75$ rpm

7. B
Call the input gear G_1 and the output gear G_2. Call the speed of G_1, S_1 and the number of teeth T_1. Similarly for G_2, we have S_2 and T_2.

Given data
S_1 = 50
T_1 = 100
S_2 = unknown
T_2 = 20

We know that $S_1 \times T_1 = S_2 \times T_2$

So, $50 \times 100 = S_2 \times 20$
$S_2 = 5000/20 = 250$ rpm

8. B
Notice the weight is attached to one end of the rope and to one pulley. The force required to lift a 100 pound weight with this arrangement is 100/3 = 33.

9. A
A robertson screwdriver would be used.

10. C
50 pounds of force much be exerted downward on the rope to lift the 200 pound weight. Since there are 4 pulleys, each will take 1/4 of the load. 200/4 = 50 pounds.

11. B
Up-and-down or back-and-forth motion is called reciprocal motion.

12. B
To solve for F, Weight X b (distance from fulcrum to weight) = Force X a (distance from fulcrum to point where force is

applied)
80 X 10 = F X 20
800/20 = F
F =40

13. A
The wheel of a pulley turning is an example of torque. Torque, moment or moment of force, is the tendency of a force to rotate an object about an axis, fulcrum, or pivot. Just as a force is a push or a pull, a torque can be thought of as a twist to an object. [12]

14. A
Choice B shows the garage on the wrong side. Choice does not show the bay window. Choice D does not show the second dormer.

15. A
The north-south width of the house pictured is 124 ft.

16. A
The east-west length of the house is 200 ft.

17. D
Choice A has the porch and the garage on the wrong side. The porch and side bay window on the right hand corner are incorrect. Choice C has the garage on the wrong side and the left hand side profile incorrect. Choice D has the front porch incorrect.

18. A
The colors of the two square boxes are reversed.

19. D
There are 4 hydrants on Indian Rd.

20. A
Choice A is the most direct route with the fewest turns. Choice B exits from the west airport exit, not the east. Choice C involves more turns and a number of short turns and exits from highways. Choice A is the best answer.

21. C
It is about 5 miles from the corner of Scottsdale Rd. and Thomas Rd. to the corder of Central Ave. and Thomas Rd.

22. B
Each figure is created by adding the mirror image of the previous figure.

23. B
Each square has 2 blank squares. Note there is a difference between a blank square and an empty area.

24. D

25. A

Practice Test Questions Set 2

THE PRACTICE TEST PORTION PRESENTS QUESTIONS THAT ARE REPRESENTATIVE OF THE TYPE OF QUESTION YOU SHOULD EXPECT TO FIND ON THE CANADIAN FIREFIGHTER EXAM. **The questions here are for skill practice only.**

For the best results, take this Practice Test as if it were the real exam. Set aside time when you will not be disturbed, and a location that is quiet and free of distractions. Read the instructions carefully, read each question carefully, and answer to the best of your ability.

Use the bubble answer sheets provided. When you have completed the Practice Test, check your answer against the Answer Key and read the explanation provided.

Reading Comprehension Answer Sheet

	A	B	C	D	E		A	B	C	D	E
1	○	○	○	○	○	21	○	○	○	○	○
2	○	○	○	○	○	22	○	○	○	○	○
3	○	○	○	○	○	23	○	○	○	○	○
4	○	○	○	○	○	24	○	○	○	○	○
5	○	○	○	○	○	25	○	○	○	○	○
6	○	○	○	○	○	26	○	○	○	○	○
7	○	○	○	○	○	27	○	○	○	○	○
8	○	○	○	○	○	28	○	○	○	○	○
9	○	○	○	○	○	29	○	○	○	○	○
10	○	○	○	○	○	30	○	○	○	○	○
11	○	○	○	○	○						
12	○	○	○	○	○						
13	○	○	○	○	○						
14	○	○	○	○	○						
15	○	○	○	○	○						
16	○	○	○	○	○						
17	○	○	○	○	○						
18	○	○	○	○	○						
19	○	○	○	○	○						
20	○	○	○	○	○						

Listening Comprehension Answer Sheet

	A	B	C	D
1	○	○	○	○
2	○	○	○	○
3	○	○	○	○
4	○	○	○	○
5	○	○	○	○
6	○	○	○	○
7	○	○	○	○
8	○	○	○	○
9	○	○	○	○
10	○	○	○	○
11	○	○	○	○
12	○	○	○	○
13	○	○	○	○
14	○	○	○	○
15	○	○	○	○
16	○	○	○	○
17	○	○	○	○
18	○	○	○	○
19	○	○	○	○
20	○	○	○	○

Mathematics Answer Sheet

	A	B	C	D	E			A	B	C	D	E
1	○	○	○	○	○		21	○	○	○	○	○
2	○	○	○	○	○		22	○	○	○	○	○
3	○	○	○	○	○		23	○	○	○	○	○
4	○	○	○	○	○		24	○	○	○	○	○
5	○	○	○	○	○		25	○	○	○	○	○
6	○	○	○	○	○		26	○	○	○	○	○
7	○	○	○	○	○		27	○	○	○	○	○
8	○	○	○	○	○		28	○	○	○	○	○
9	○	○	○	○	○		29	○	○	○	○	○
10	○	○	○	○	○		30	○	○	○	○	○
11	○	○	○	○	○							
12	○	○	○	○	○							
13	○	○	○	○	○							
14	○	○	○	○	○							
15	○	○	○	○	○							
16	○	○	○	○	○							
17	○	○	○	○	○							
18	○	○	○	○	○							
19	○	○	○	○	○							
20	○	○	○	○	○							

Mechanical Aptitude Answer Sheet

	A	B	C	D	E		A	B	C	D	E
1	○	○	○	○	○	21	○	○	○	○	○
2	○	○	○	○	○	22	○	○	○	○	○
3	○	○	○	○	○	23	○	○	○	○	○
4	○	○	○	○	○	24	○	○	○	○	○
5	○	○	○	○	○	25	○	○	○	○	○
6	○	○	○	○	○	26	○	○	○	○	○
7	○	○	○	○	○	27	○	○	○	○	○
8	○	○	○	○	○	28	○	○	○	○	○
9	○	○	○	○	○	29	○	○	○	○	○
10	○	○	○	○	○	30	○	○	○	○	○
11	○	○	○	○	○						
12	○	○	○	○	○						
13	○	○	○	○	○						
14	○	○	○	○	○						
15	○	○	○	○	○						
16	○	○	○	○	○						
17	○	○	○	○	○						
18	○	○	○	○	○						
19	○	○	○	○	○						
20	○	○	○	○	○						

Reading Comprehension

Questions 1 - 4 refer to the following passage.

Passage 1 - The Crusades

In 1095 Pope Urban II proclaimed the First Crusade with the intent and stated goal to restore Christian access to holy places in and around Jerusalem. Over the next 200 years there were 6 major crusades and numerous minor crusades in the fight for control of the "Holy Land." Historians are divided on the real purpose of the Crusades, some believing that it was part of a purely defensive war against Islamic conquest; some see them as part of a long-running conflict at the frontiers of Europe; and others see them as confident, aggressive, papal-led expansion attempts by Western Christendom. The impact of the crusades was profound, and judgment of the Crusaders ranges from laudatory to highly critical. However, all agree that the Crusades and wars waged during those crusades were brutal and often bloody. Several hundred thousand Roman Catholic Christians joined the Crusades, they were Christians from all over Europe.

Europe at the time was under the Feudal System, so while the Crusaders made vows to the Church, they also were beholden to their Feudal Lords. This led to the Crusaders not only fighting the Saracen, the commonly used word for Muslim at the time, but also each other for power and economic gain in the Holy Land. This infighting between the Crusaders is why many historians hold the view that the Crusades were simply a front for Europe to invade the Holy Land for economic gain in the name of the Church. Another factor contributing to this theory is that while the army of crusaders marched towards Jerusalem they pillaged the land as they went. The church and feudal Lords vowing to return the land to its original beauty, and inhabitants, this rarely happened though, as the Lords often kept the land for themselves. A full 800 years after the Crusades, Pope John Paul II expressed his sorrow for the massacre of innocent people and the lasting damage that the Medieval church caused in that area of the World.

Practice Test Questions 2

1. What is the tone of this article?

    a. Subjective

    b. Objective

    c. Persuasive

    d. None of the Above

2. What can all historians agree on concerning the Crusades?

    a. It achieved great things

    b. It stabilized the Holy Land

    c. It was bloody and brutal

    d. It helped defend Europe from the Byzantine Empire

3. What impact did the feudal system have on the Crusades

    a. It unified the Crusaders

    b. It helped gather volunteers

    c. It had no effect on the Crusades

    d. It led to infighting, causing more damage than good

4. What does Saracen mean?

    a. Muslim

    b. Christian

    c. Knight

    d. Holy Land

Questions 5 - 8 refer to the following passage.

ABC Electric Warranty

ABC Electric Company warrants that its products are free from defects in material and workmanship. Subject to the conditions and limitations set forth below, ABC Electric will, at its option, either repair or replace any part of its products that prove defective due to improper workmanship or materials.

This limited warranty does not cover any damage to the product from improper installation, accident, abuse, misuse, natural disaster, insufficient or excessive electrical supply, abnormal mechanical or environmental conditions, or any unauthorized disassembly, repair, or modification.

This limited warranty also does not apply to any product on which the original identification information has been altered, or removed, has not been handled or packaged correctly, or has been sold as second-hand.

This limited warranty covers only repair, replacement, refund or credit for defective ABC Electric products, as provided above.

5. I tried to repair my ABC Electric blender, but could not, so can I get it repaired under this warranty?

    a. Yes, the warranty still covers the blender

    b. No, the warranty does not cover the blender

    c. Uncertain. ABC Electric may or may not cover repairs under this warranty

6. My ABC Electric fan is not working. Will ABC Electric provide a new one or repair this one?

    a. ABC Electric will repair my fan

    b. ABC Electric will replace my fan

    c. ABC Electric could either replace or repair my fan can request either a replacement or a repair.

7. My stove was damaged in a flood. Does this warranty cover my stove?

    a. Yes, it is covered.

    b. No, it is not covered.

    c. It may or may not be covered.

    d. ABC Electric will decide if it is covered

8. Which of the following is an example of improper workmanship?

    a. Missing parts

    b. Defective parts

    c. Scratches on the front

    d. None of the above

Questions 9 – 12 refer to the following passage.

Passage 2 - Women and Advertising

Only in the last few generations have media messages been so widespread and so readily seen, heard, and read by so many people. Advertising is an important part of both selling and buying anything from soap to cereal to jeans. For whatever reason, more consumers are women than are men. Media message are subtle but powerful, and more attention has been paid lately to how these message affect women. Of all the products that women buy, makeup, clothes, and other stylistic or cosmetic products are among the most popular. This means that companies focus their advertising on women, promising them that their product will make her feel, look, or smell better than the next company's product will. This competition has resulted in advertising that is more and more ideal and less and less possible for everyday women. However, because women do look to these ideals and the products they represent as how they can potentially become, many women have developed unhealthy attitudes about themselves when they have failed to become those ideals.

In recent years, more companies have tried to change advertisements to be healthier for women. This includes featuring models of more sizes and addressing a huge outcry against unfair tools such as airbrushing and photo editing. There is debate about what the right balance between real and ideal is, because fashion is also considered art and some changes are made to purposefully elevate fashionable products and signify that they are creative, innovative, and the work of individual people. Artists want their freedom protected as much as women do, and advertising agencies are often caught in the middle.

Some claim that the companies who make these changes are not doing enough. Many people worry that there are still not enough models of different sizes and different ethnicities. Some people claim that companies use this healthier type of advertisement not for the good of women, but because they would like to sell products to the women who are looking for these kinds of messages. This is also a hard balance to find: companies need to make money, and women need to feel respected.

While the focus of this change has been on women, advertising can also affect men, and this change will hopefully be a lesson on media for all consumers.

9. The second paragraph states that advertising focuses on women

    a. to shape what the ideal should be

    b. because women buy makeup

    c. because women are easily persuaded

    d. because of the types of products that women buy

10. According to the passage, fashion artists and female consumers are at odds because

    a. there is a debate going on and disagreement drives people apart

    b. both of them are trying to protect their freedom to do something

    c. artists want to elevate their products above the reach of women

    d. women are creative, innovative, individual people

11. The author uses the phrase "for whatever reason" in this passage to

    a. keep the focus of the paragraph on media messages and not on the differences between men and women

    b. show that the reason for this is unimportant

    c. argue that it is stupid that more women are consumers than men

    d. show that he or she is tired of talking about why media messages are important

12. This passage suggests that

    a. advertising companies are still working on making their messages better

    b. all advertising companies seek to be more approachable for women

    c. women are only buying from companies that respect them

    d. artists could stop producing fashionable products if they feel bullied

Questions 13 - 16 refer to the following passage.

FDR, the Treaty of Versailles, and the Fourteen Points

At the conclusion of World War I, those who had won the war and those who were forced to admit defeat welcomed the end of the war and expected that a peace treaty would be signed. The American president, Franklin D. Roosevelt, played an important part in proposing what the agreements should be and did so through his Fourteen Points.
World War I had begun in 1914 when an Austrian archduke was assassinated, leading to a domino effect that pulled the world's most powerful countries into war on a large scale. The war catalysed the creation and use of deadly weapons that had not previously existed, resulting in a great loss of soldiers on both sides of the fighting. More than 9 million soldiers were killed.

The United States agreed to enter the war right before it ended, and many believed that its decision to become finally involved brought on the end of the war. FDR made it very clear that the U.S. was entering the war for moral reasons and had an agenda focused on world peace. The Fourteen Points were individual goals and ideas (focused on peace, free trade, open communication, and self-reliance) that FDR wanted the power nations to strive for now that the war had ended. He was optimistic and had many ideas about what could be accomplished through, and during the post-war peace. However, FDR's fourteen points were poorly received when he presented them to the leaders of other world powers, many of whom wanted only to help their own countries and to punish the Germans for fueling the war, and they fell by the wayside. World War II was imminent, for Germany lost everything.

Some historians believe that the other leaders who participated in the Treaty of Versailles weren't receptive to the Fourteen Points because World War I was fought almost entirely on European soil, and the United States lost much less than did the other powers. FDR was in a unique position to determine the fate of the war, but doing it on his own terms did not help accomplish his goals. This is only one historical example of how the United State has tried to use its power as an important country, but found itself limited because of geological or ideological factors.

13. The main idea of this passage is that

a. World War I was unfair because no fighting took place in America

b. World War II happened because of the Treaty of Versailles

c. the power the United States has to help other countries also prevents it from helping other countries

d. Franklin D. Roosevelt was one of the United States' smartest presidents

14. According to the second paragraph, World War I started because

a. an archduke was assassinated

b. weapons that were more deadly had been developed

c. a domino effect of allies agreeing to help each other

d. the world's most powerful countries were large

15. The author includes the detail that 9 million soldiers were killed

a. to demonstrate why European leaders were hesitant to accept peace

b. to show the reader the dangers of deadly weapons

c. to make the reader think about which countries lost the most soldiers

d. to demonstrate why World War II was imminent

16. According to this passage, catalysed means

    a. analyzed
    b. sped up
    c. invented
    d. funded

Questions 17 - 20 refer to the following passage.

Chocolate Chip Cookies

3/4 cup sugar
3/4 cup packed brown sugar
1 cup butter, softened
2 large eggs, beaten
1 teaspoon vanilla extract
2 1/4 cups all-purpose flour
1 teaspoon baking soda
3/4 teaspoon salt
2 cups semisweet chocolate chips
If desired, 1 cup chopped pecans, or chopped walnuts.
Preheat oven to 375 degrees.

Mix sugar, brown sugar, butter, vanilla and eggs in a large bowl. Stir in flour, baking soda, and salt. The dough will be very stiff.

Stir in chocolate chips by hand with a sturdy wooden spoon. Add the pecans, or other nuts, if desired. Stir until the chocolate chips and nuts are evenly dispersed.

Drop dough by rounded tablespoonfuls 2 inches apart onto a cookie sheet.

Bake 8 to 10 minutes, or, until light brown. Cookies may look underdone, but they will finish cooking after you take them out of the oven.

17. What is the correct order for adding these ingredi-

ents?

 a. Brown sugar, baking soda, chocolate chips
 b. Baking soda, brown sugar, chocolate chips
 c. Chocolate chips, baking soda, brown sugar
 d. Baking soda, chocolate chips, brown sugar

18. What does sturdy mean?

 a. Long
 b. Strong
 c. Short
 d. Wide

19. What does disperse mean?

 a. Scatter
 b. To form a ball
 c. To stir
 d. To beat

20. When can you stop stirring the nuts?

 a. When the cookies are cooked.
 b. When the nuts are evenly distributed.
 c. When the nuts are added.
 d. After the chocolate chips are added.

Questions 21 - 24 refer to the following passage.

Lowest Price Guarantee

Get it for less. Guaranteed!

ABC Electric will beat any advertised price by 10% of the difference.

1) If you find a lower advertised price, we will beat it by 10% of the difference.

2) If you find a lower advertised price within 30 days* of your purchase we will beat it by 10% of the difference.

3) If our own price is reduced within 30 days* of your purchase, bring in your receipt and we will refund the difference.

*14 days for computers, monitors, printers, laptops, tablets, cellular & wireless devices, home security products, projectors, camcorders, digital cameras, radar detectors, portable DVD players, DJ and pro-audio equipment, and air conditioners.

21. I bought a radar detector 15 days ago and saw an ad for the same model only cheaper. Can I get 10% of the difference refunded?

    a. Yes. Since it is less than 30 days, you can get 10% of the difference refunded.

    b. No. Since it is more than 14 days, you cannot get 10% of the difference re-funded.

    c. It depends on the cashier.

    d. Yes. You can get the difference refunded.

22. I bought a flat-screen TV for $500 10 days ago and found an advertisement for the same TV, at another store, on sale for $400. How much will ABC refund under this guarantee?

    a. $100

    b. $110

    c. $10

    d. $400

23. What is the purpose of this passage?

    a. To inform
    b. To educate
    c. To persuade
    d. To entertain

Questions 24 - 26 refer to the following passage.

Passage 6 - What Is Mardi Gras?

Mardi Gras is fast becoming one of the South's most famous and most celebrated holidays. The word Mardi Gras comes from the French and the literal translation is "Fat Tuesday." The holiday has also been called Shrove Tuesday, due to its associations with Lent. The purpose of Mardi Gras is to celebrate and enjoy before the Lenten season of fasting and repentance begins.

What originated by the French Explorers in New Orleans, Louisiana in the 17th century is now celebrated all over the world. Panama, Italy, Belgium and Brazil all host large scale Mardi Gras celebrations, and many smaller cities and towns celebrate this fun loving Tuesday as well. Usually held in February or early March, Mardi Gras is a day of extravagance, a day for people to eat, drink and be merry, to wear costumes, masks and to dance to jazz music.
The French explorers on the Mississippi River would be in shock today if they saw the opulence of the parades and floats that grace the New Orleans streets during Mardi Gras these days. Parades in New Orleans are divided by organizations. These are more commonly known as Krewes.

Being a member of a Krewe is quite a task because Krewes are responsible for overseeing the parades. Each Krewe's parade is ruled by a Mardi Gras "King and Queen." The role of the King and Queen is to "bestow" gifts on their adoring fans as the floats ride along the street. They throw doubloons, which is fake money and usually colored green, purple and gold, which are the colors of Mardi Gras. Beads in those color shades are also thrown and cups are thrown as well. Beads are by far the most popular souvenir of any Mardi Gras parade, with each spectator attempting to gather as many as possible.

24. The purpose of Mardi Gras is to

    a. Repent for a month.

    b. Celebrate in extravagant ways.

    c. Be a member of a Krewe.

    d. Explore the Mississippi.

25. From reading the passage we can infer that "Kings and Queens"

    a. Have to be members of a Krewe.

    b. Have to be French.

    c. Have to know how to speak French.

    d. Have to give away their own money.

26. Which group of people began to hold Mardi Gras celebrations?

    a. Settlers from Italy

    b. Members of Krewes

    c. French explorers

    d. Belgium explorers

27. In the context of the passage, what does the word spectator mean?

    a. Someone who participates actively

    b. Someone who watches the parade's action

    c. Someone on the parade floats

    d. Someone who does not celebrate Mardi Gras

Questions 28 - 30 refer to the following passage.

Passage 7 - Firefighters

Firefighters are rescuers trained to put out any type of fire. There are fire departments in almost every country in the world, and they are one of the three main emergency services, along with the police department and the emergency medical services.

Firefighters receive extensive training in fire fighting to assure that they are prepared to handle any situation. While on duty, firemen or firewomen might have to deal with fire prevention, fire suppression, ventilation, containment, search and rescue, and many others.

The main goal of the fire departments is to save lives, protect property, and protect the environment from the dangers of a big fire. Traditionally, the firefighters are associated with Dalmatians as helper animals. While most fire departments use dogs, they are not Dalmatians. Fire departments only used dogs for rescue operations, and keep them away from fires.

28. What are the three main emergency services?

    a. fire department, emergency medical and police

    b. fire departments, emergency medical and highway patrol

    c. RCMP, fire departments and emergency medical

    d. Disaster relief, fire departments, and emergency medical

29. What are the main goals of the fire department?

    a. put out fires and protect property

    b. to save lives, protect property and protect the environment

    c. to save lives, put out fires and protect property

    d. to protect property, save the environment and put out fires

30. What animal is traditionally associated with firefighters?

    a. Dogs

    b. Dalmatians

    c. Horses

    d. No animals are associated with firefighters

Part II - Listening Comprehension

Directions: Scan the QR code below with any smartphone or tablet for an audio recording of the listening comprehension passages below. Or, have someone read them to you. Listen carefully to the passages and answer the questions that follow.

What is a QR Code?
A QR code looks like a barcode and it's used as a shortcut to link to content online using your phone's camera, saving you from typing lengthy addresses into your mobile browser.

Questions 1 - 3 refer to the following passage.

Passage 1 - Common Causes of household fires

It's hard to believe, but the most common causes of house fires are the most common things in houses. This is because we use fire, or electricity daily, as part of our regular routine; cooking, heating water in water heaters, decorative candles and in many other ways. Another thing people don't usually consider is that electrical failures can cause a fire.

Most fires start in the kitchen when a pot on the stove is left unattended. Even something as simple as a pot with boiling water can be dangerous: if the water spills from the pot and extinguishes the fire in the burner, and the propane gas spreads through the kitchen. After this, it only needs a spark to start a fire.

If there is someone there that can turn off the gas, or get the burner going again, there will be no hazard. So, the kitchen mustn't be left unattended as a precaution.

Electricity can cause a fire in many ways; an electrical short, a damaged wire, an overloaded power circuit, an over-heated hair dryer or even for poor installation of equipment. So, it's important to make every installation properly done and that they get adequate maintenance. Poor installation of house wiring can be especially dangerous. Therefore there are so many regulations regarding the electrical installation.

Smoking is another major cause of fires. A cigarette in bed can light the sheets and start a fire, a half-burned but falling on the carpet can also start a fire.

Scan for Audio or click
https://www.test-preparation.ca/audio/HouseHoldFires.mp3

1. Why are household fires so common?

    a. Faulty wiring

    b. Because we use fire so often

    c. Household fires are not common

    d. A lot of people smoke

2. Where so most fires start?

    a. the kitchen

    b. the bedroom

    c. the living room

    d. the basement

3. **What is a major cause of fires besides electricity and fire?**

   a. Power tools
   b. Smoking
   c. Pets
   d. Laptops

Questions 4 - 6 refer to the following passage.

News story #1

This weekend a home in Brooklyn burst into flames while the owners where downtown. The young couple, Mary and John Smith left their home Saturday morning, after a quick breakfast, and went downtown to spend the day. But the day was interrupted at noon by a call from the couples' upstairs neighbor, who said that he smelled smoke, called the fire department, and that their apartment was in flames. When Mary and John got home, the fire department had put out the fire, and there was only ashes.

The preliminary assessment of the fire department indicated the fire was started by candles left on a desk, near papers on a big bookshelf. Also, the department had no fire security system to warn of the smoke. The regulations regarding home fire security stated that lit candles can't be left unattended, so the fire department declared the fire was causes by negligence. With this, the insurance company can deny to responsibility in the terrible accident.

Scan for audio or click
https://www.test-preparation.ca/audio/News1.mp3

4. Where were the owners when the fire started?

   a. At home

   b. Visiting their friend upstairs

   c. Downtown for the day

   d. In the backyard

5. What started the fire?

   a. Candles left burning near some papers

   b. We don't know the cause

   c. The flames started from cooking breakfast

   d. The upstairs neighbor

6. Did their home burn down completely?

   a. Yes

   b. No

   c. We cannot tell from the story

Questions 7 - 9 refer to the following passage.

News story #2

This is a story about a hero without a cape: an 18-year-old boy rescued a baby and an elderly woman from a burning house.

On his way to school Tom Pitt noticed smoke coming out of a house near his home. As he approached the smoking house, he noticed that the house was on fire and heard screams coming from the inside. The teenager immediately called the emergency service and gave the address. But the house is a bit outside the city, so he knew that it would take a while before the fire department got there.

The young hero ran into the blazing house, rescuing a one-year old baby girl and then coming back to rescue her 83-year-old grandmother. They were trapped inside the fire, which presumably started because the granny fell asleep, leaving the oven ON. The young hero, Tom Pitt, was awarded with the keys to the city for his amazing rescue, risking his life to save others.

Scan for audio or click
https://www.test-preparation.ca/audio/News2.mp3

11. Where was Tom going when he noticed the burning house?

    a. He was at home

    b. He was going to school

    c. He was going home

    d. He was going downtown

12. What did Tom do when he saw the house was on fire?

    a. He went into rescue the baby and grandmother

    b. He called the emergency services

    c. He went home to call the emergency services

    d. None of the above

13. Why did it take a long time for the firefighters to arrive?

    a. The fire department was busy

    b. It did not take a long time

    c. I take a long time because the house was out of town

    c. None of the above

Questions 14 - 15 refer to the following passage.

Volcanoes

A volcano is a split in the plates that compose the surface of a planet. A split in the plates, allows gases, lava and volcanic ashes in magma chambers deep below the Earth to surface, when the volcano erupts. There are many volcanoes on planet Earth. Most volcanos are underwater. Volcanoes are the natural way that the Earth has of releasing internal heat and pressure. A volcano erupts when the pressure of the magma below the surface is greater than the rocks surrounding it.

Scan for audio or click
https://www.test-preparation.ca/audio/Volcano.mp3

14. Where are most volcanoes?

    a. Underwater

    b. On land

    c. In Europe

    d. In the US

15. What causes volcanoes?

   a. Magma
   b. A split in the earth's plates
   c. Escaping gas
   c. None of the above

Questions 16 - 19 refer to the following passage.

Types of Volcanoes

One of the biggest tragedies in the history of mankind occurred when the volcano Vesuvius erupted and covered The roman city of Pompeii with lava and toxic gases in minutes. But despite its dangers, they are a necessary process that the Earth uses to balance itself.

There are many types of volcanoes, many are underwater, others over the surface; some have constant small eruptions, some other haven't erupted in centuries; some have conical form, others are narrow. For example, shield volcanoes are common in the Hawaiian volcanic chain. Shield volcanoes are volcanoes with small explosions of a low-viscosity lava that can flow long distances. There are also volcanoes called lava domes. Unlike shield volcanoes, these have highly viscous lava that covers the mountain. There are as well Stratovolcanoes, which are tall conical mountains formed of lava flows, so they are shaped during different eruptions.

The terrible super-volcanoes are capable of destruction on a continental scale. Due to the enormous volume of ashes and sulfuric vapors, they can even cool the global temperature for years after the eruption. Underwater volcanoes are very common on the ocean floor. They don't usually have big explosions due to the enormous weight and pressure of the water, which prevents the gases from being released.

Practice Test Questions 2

Scan for audio or click
https://www.test-preparation.ca/audio/TypesVolcano.mp3

16. What happened when Vesuvius erupted?

   a. It covered the city of Pompeii
   b. It cooled the global temperature
   c. It was not a big explosion
   d. None of the above

17. Where are Shield Volcanoes commonly found?

   a. In the Arctic
   b. In Russia
   c. In the Hawaiian Islands
   d. In Canada

18. What are Stratovolcanoes?

   a. Super-volcanoes
   b. Conical mountains of lava
   c. Underwater volcanoes
   d. Lava domes

19. Do underwater volcanoes have big explosions?

   a. Yes
   b. No

Question 20 refers to the following passage.

Wild Animals in Urban Areas

In this last decade, the presence of wild animals in the cities has increased dramatically. in Germany wolves are now commonly seen in suburban areas, in Los Angeles mountain lions are frequently found in backyards, and in London the presence of deer in urban areas is more and more common. There are several theories to explain this curious phenomenon. Many scientists believe the main reason of the increased presence of wild animals in urban areas is human invasion of the natural habitat. Therefore, it's not them coming to us, instead it's us going to them.

This phenomenon is not new, wild life had cohabited with humans since ancient times. When cities grew bigger and industrialized, wildlife was rarely seen. Now, wildlife has returned to urban areas. So, to animals, this is more like a return to the cities than an invasion. To most urban dwelling people today, contact with wild life seems unimaginable, but really it is not new!

Scan for audio or click
https://www.test-preparation.ca/audio/WildlifeUrban.mp3

20. What is commonly found in Los Angeles backyards?

    a. Deer
    b. Mountain Lions
    c. Wolves
    d. Rabbits

Part III – Math

1. 8327 – 1278 =

   a. 7149
   b. 7209
   c. 6059
   d. 7049

2. 294 X 21 =

   a. 6017
   b. 6174
   c. 6728
   d. 5679

3. 1278 + 4920 =

   a. 6298
   b. 6108
   c. 6198
   d. 6098

4. 285 * 12 =

   a. 3420
   b. 3402
   c. 3024
   d. 2322

5. 4120 – 3216 =

    a. 903
    b. 804
    c. 904
    d. 1904

6. 2417 + 1004 =

    a. 3401
    b. 4321
    c. 3402
    d. 3421

7. 1440 ÷ 12 =

    a. 122
    b. 120
    c. 110
    d. 132

8. 2713 – 1308 =

    a. 1450
    b. 1445
    c. 1405
    d. 1455

9. The length of a rectangle is 5 in. more than its width. The perimeter of the rectangle is 26 in. What is the width and length of the rectangle?

    a. width = 6 inches, Length = 9 inches
    b. width = 4 inches, Length = 9 inches
    c. width =4 inches, Length = 5 inches
    d. width = 6 inches, Length = 11 inches

10. Kate's father is 32 years older than Kate is. In 5 years, he will be five times older. How old is Kate?

    a. 2
    b. 3
    c. 5
    d. 6

11. A store owner buys merchandise for $21,045. He transports them for $3,905 and pays his staff $1,450 to stock the merchandise on his shelves. If he does not incur further costs, how much does he need to sell the items to make $5,000 profit?

    a. $32,500
    b. $29,350
    c. $32,400
    d. $31,400

12. A basket contains 125 oranges, mangos and apples. If 3/5 of the fruits in the basket are mangos and only 2/5 of the mangos are ripe, how many ripe mangos are there in the basket?

    a. 30
    b. 68
    c. 55
    d. 47

13. Employees of a discount appliance store receive an additional 20% off the lowest price on any item. If an employee purchases a dishwasher during a 15% off sale, how much will he pay if the dishwasher originally cost $450?

    a. $280.90
    b. $287.00
    c. $292.50
    d. $306.00

14. The sale price of a car is $12,590, which is 20% off the original price. What is the original price?

    a. $14,310.40
    b. $14,990.90
    c. $15,108.00
    d. $15,737.50

15. A goat eats 214 kg. of hay in 60 days, while a cow eats the same amount in 15 days. How long will it take them to eat this hay together?

    a. 37.5
    b. 75
    c. 12
    d. 15

16. Express 25% as a fraction.

    a. 1/4
    b. 7/40
    c. 6/25
    d. 8/28

17. Express 125% as a decimal.

    a. .125
    b. 12.5
    c. 1.25
    d. 125

18. Solve for x: 30 is 40% of x

   a. 60
   b. 90
   c. 85
   d. 75

19. 12 ½% of x is equal to 50. Solve for x.

   a. 300
   b. 400
   c. 450
   d. 350

20. Express 24/56 as a reduced common fraction.

   a. 4/9
   b. 4/11
   c. 3/7
   d. 3/8

21. Express 87% as a decimal.

   a. .087
   b. 8.7
   c. .87
   d. 87

22. 60 is 75% of x. Solve for x.

   a. 80
   b. 90
   c. 75
   d. 70

23. 60% of x is 12. Solve for x.

    a. 18
    b. 15
    c. 25
    d. 20

24. Express 71/1000 as a decimal.

    a. .71
    b. .0071
    c. .071
    d. 7.1

25. 4.7 + .9 + .01 =

    a. 5.5
    b. 6.51
    c. 5.61
    d. 5.7

26. .84 ÷ .7 =

    a. .12
    b. 12
    c. .012
    d. 1.2

27. What number is in the ten thousandths place in 1.7389?

    a. 1
    b. 8
    c. 9
    d. 3

28. .87 - .48 =

    a. .39

    b. .49

    c. .41

    d. .37

29. Convert 60 feet to inches.

    a. 700 inches

    b. 600 inches

    c. 720 inches

    d. 1,800 inches

30. Convert 25 centimeters to millimeters.

    a. 250 millimeters

    b. 7.5 millimeters

    c. 5 millimeters

    d. 2.5 millimeters

Part IV - Mechanical Comprehension

1. Which of the following is true of the relationship between screws and threads?

    a. The larger the distance between threads, the easier to turn.

    b. The smaller the distance between threads, the easier to turn.

    c. The smaller the distance between threads, the more difficult to turn.

    d. None of the above

2. Consider the arrangement of pulleys above. If the weight shown is 150 pounds, how much force much be exerted to lift the weight?

    a. 150 pounds
    b. 100 pounds
    c. 75 pounds
    d. 50 pounds

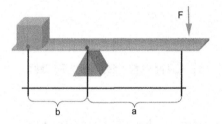

3. Consider the illustration above and the corresponding data:

Weight = W = 100 pounds
Distance from fulcrum to Weight = b = 5 feet
Distance from fulcrum to point where force is applied = a = 10 feet

How much force (F) must be applied to lift the weight?

   a. 100
   b. 50
   c. 25
   d. 10

4. Consider a gear train with 3 gears, from left to right, A with 10 teeth, gear B with 40 teeth, and gear C with 10 teeth. Gear A turns clockwise at 80 rpm. What direction and speed in rpm does Gear C turn?

   a. 100 rpm, clockwise
   b. 80 rpm clockwise
   c. 120 rpm counter clockwise
   d. 100 rpm counter clockwise

5. Consider the pulley arrangement above. If the weight, W, is 100 pounds, then how much force is required to lift the weight?

   a. 100 pounds
   b. 50 pounds
   c. 25 pounds
   d. 20 pounds

6. A cam is a mechanical linkage that:

   a. Transforms linear motion into rotary motion and vice versa.

   b. Transforms oscillating motion in to linear motion and vice versa.

   c. Transforms reciprocating motion to oscillating motion.

   d. None of the above

7. What is the function of a crankshaft?

   a. To transform the back-and-forth motion of the pistons into rotary motion.

   b. To transform rotary motion into reciprocal motion.

   c. To transfer the rotary motion of the cam to the wheels

   d. None of the above.

8. Consider two meshed gears, one that is twice as large as the other. How fast will the smaller gear rotate?

   a. One-quarter as fast as the larger gear

   b. Twice as fast as the larger gear

   c. 50% faster than the larger gear

   d. None of the above

9. What does a tachometer measure?

   a. A tachometer measures rotation speed

   b. A tachometer measures temperature

   c. A tachometer measures pressure

   d. A tachometer measures speed

10. Which of the following best describes an allen wrench?
   a. An l-shaped wrench with 5 sides
   b. An l-shaped wrench with 6 sides
   c. An l-shaped wrench with 4 sides
   d. None of the above

11. What tool is used to tighten bits in an electric drill?
   a. Chuck
   b. Tang
   c. Allen Wrench
   d. None of the above

12. How many hydrants are on Los Feliz Blvd?
   a. 1
   b. 2
   c. 3
   d. 4

13. Taking the shortest route from Golden State Fwy 5 and Los Felix, to Santa Monica Blvd and Versont, how many corners are there?

    a. 1
    b. 2
    c. 3
    d. 4

14. What is the width of this house from west to east?

    a. 47
    b. 37
    c. 46
    d. 48

15. What is the length of this house from north to south?

    a. 47
    b. 37
    c. 46
    d. 48

16. Which of the following represent an overhead view of the house below?

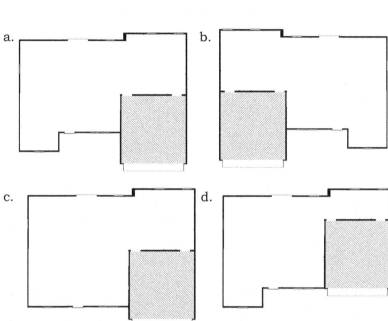

17. Which of the following represent an overhead view of the house below?

a.

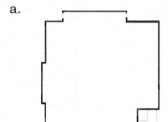

b.

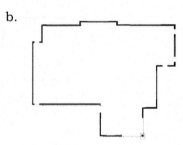

c.

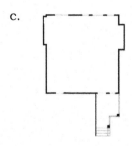

d.

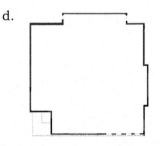

18.

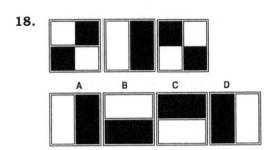

19. When folded into a loop, what will the strip of paper look like?

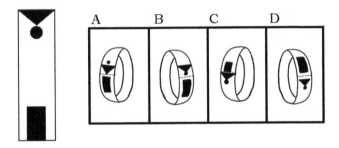

20. Which of the choices is the same pattern at a different angle?

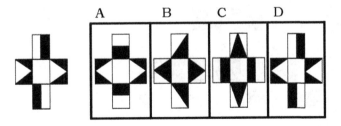

21. When put together, what 3-dimensional shape will you get?

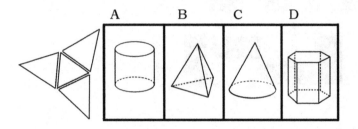

22. Choose to complete the sequence.

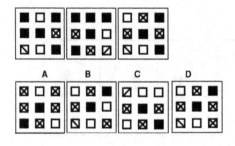

23. Choose to complete the sequence.

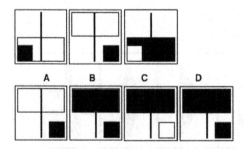

24. Choose to complete the sequence.

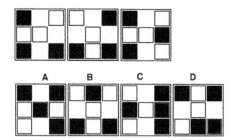

25. Choose to complete the sequence.

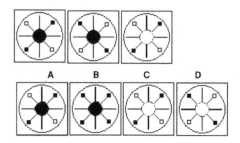

Answer Key

1. A
Choice B is incorrect; the author did not express their opinion on the subject matter. Choice C is incorrect, the author was not trying to prove a point.

2. C
Choice C is correct; historians believe it was brutal and bloody. Choice A is incorrect; there is no consensus that the Crusades achieved great things. Choice B is incorrect; it did not stabilize the Holy Lands. Choice D is incorrect, some historians do believe this was the purpose but not all historians.

3. D
The feudal system led to infighting. Choice A is incorrect, it had the opposite effect. Choice B is incorrect, though this is a good answer, it is not the best answer. The Church asked for volunteers not the Feudal Lords. Choice C is incorrect, it did have an effect on the Crusades.

4. A
Saracen was a generic term for Muslims widely used in Europe during the later medieval era.

5. B
This warranty does not cover a product that you have tried to fix yourself. From paragraph two, "This limited warranty does not cover … any unauthorized disassembly, repair, or modification. "

6. C
ABC Electric could either replace or repair the fan, provided the other conditions are met. ABC Electric has the option to repair or replace.

7. B
The warranty does not cover a stove damaged in a flood. From the passage, "This limited warranty does not cover any damage to the product from improper installation, accident, abuse, misuse, natural disaster, insufficient or excessive electrical supply, abnormal mechanical or environmental

conditions."

A flood is an "abnormal environmental condition," and a natural disaster, so it is not covered.

8. A
A missing part is an example of defective workmanship. This is an error made in the manufacturing process. A defective part is not considered workmanship.

9. D
This question tests the reader's summarization skills. The other choices A, B, and C focus on portions of the second paragraph that are too narrow and do not relate to the specific portion of text in question. The complexity of the sentence may mislead students into selecting one of these answers, but rearranging or restating the sentence will lead the reader to the correct answer. In addition, choice A makes an assumption that may or may not be true about the intentions of the company, choice B focuses on one product rather than the idea of the products, and choice C makes an assumption about women that may or may not be true and is not supported by the text.

10. B
This question tests reader's attention to detail. If a reader selects A, he or she may have picked up on the use of the word "debate" and assumed, very logically, that the two are at odds because they are fighting; however, this is simply not supported in the text. Choice C also uses very specific quotes from the text, but it rearranges and gives them false meaning. The artists want to elevate their creations above the creations of other artists, thereby showing that they are "creative" and "innovative." Similarly, choice D takes phrases straight from the text and rearranges and confuses them. The artists are described as wanting to be "creative, innovative, individual people," not the women.

11. A
This question tests reader's vocabulary and summarization skills. This phrase, used by the author, may seem flippant and dismissive if readers focus on the word "whatever" and misinterpret it as a popular, colloquial term. In this way,

choices B and C may mislead the reader to selecting one of them by including the terms "unimportant" and "stupid," respectively. Choice D is a similar misreading, but doesn't make sense when the phrase is at the beginning of the passage and the entire passage is on media messages. Choice A is literally and contextually appropriate, and the reader can understand that the author would like to keep the introduction focused on the topic the passage is going to discuss.

12. A

This question tests a reader's inference skills. The extreme use of the word "all" in choice B suggests that every single advertising company are working to be approachable, and while this is not only unlikely, the text specifically states that "more" companies have done this, signifying that they have not all participated, even if it's a possibility that they may some day. The use of the limiting word "only" in choice C lends that answer similar problems; women are still buying from companies who do not care about this message, or those companies would not be in business, and the passage specifies that "many" women are worried about media messages, but not all. Readers may find choice D logical, especially if they are looking to make an inference, and while this may be a possibility, the passage does not suggest or discuss this happening. Choice A is correct based on specifically because of the relation between "still working" in the answer and "will hopefully" and the extensive discussion on companies struggles, which come only with progress, in the text.

13. C

This question tests the reader's summarization skills. The entire passage is leading up to the idea that the president of the US may not have had grounds to assert his Fourteen Points when other countries had lost so much. Choice A is pretty directly inferred by the text, but it does not adequately summarize what the entire passage is trying to communicate. Choice B may also be inferred by the passage when it says that the war is "imminent," but it does not represent the entire message, either. The passage does seem to be in praise of FDR, or at least in respect of him, but it does not in any way claim that he is the smartest president, nor does this represent the many other points included. Choice C is then the obvious answer, and most directly relates to the closing sentences which it rewords.

14. C

This question tests the reader's attention to detail. The passage does state that choices A and B are true, and while those statements are in proximity to the explanation for why the war started, they are not the reason given. Choice D is a mix up of words used in the passage, which says that the largest powers were in play but not that this fact somehow started the war. The passage does make a direct statement that a domino effect started the war, supporting choice C as the correct answer.

15. A

This question tests the reader's understanding of functions in writing. Throughout the passage, it states that leaders of other nations were hesitant to accept generous or peaceful terms because of the grievances of the war, and the great loss of life was chief among these. While the passage does touch on the devastation of deadly weapons (B), the use of this raw, emotional fact serves a much larger purpose, and the focus of the passage is not the weapons. While readers may indeed consider who lost the most soldiers (C) when, so many countries were involved and the inequalities of loss are mentioned in the passage, there is no discussion of this in the passage. Choice D is related to A, but choice A is more direct and relates more to the passage.

16. B

This question tests the reader's vocabulary skills. Choice A may seem appealing to readers because it is phonetically similar to "catalysed," but the two are not related in any other way. Choice C makes sense in context, but if plugged in to the sentence creates a redundancy that doesn't make sense. Choice D does also not make sense contextually, even if the reader may consider that funds were needed to create more weaponry, especially if it was advanced.

17. A

The correct order of ingredients is brown sugar, baking soda and chocolate chips.

18. B
Sturdy: strong, solid in structure or person. In context, Stir in chocolate chips by hand with a *sturdy* wooden spoon.

19. A
Disperse: to scatter in different directions or break up. In context, Stir until the chocolate chips and nuts are evenly *dispersed*.

20. B
You can stop stirring the nuts when they are evenly distributed. From the passage, "Stir until the chocolate chips and nuts are evenly dispersed."

21. B
The time limit for radar detectors is 14 days. Since you made the purchase 15 days ago, you do not qualify for the guarantee.

22. B
Since you made the purchase 10 days ago, you are covered by the guarantee. Since it is an advertised price at a different store, ABC Electric will "beat" the price by 10% of the difference, which is,

500 − 400 = 100 − difference in price

100 X 10% = $10 − 10% of the difference

The advertised lower price is $400. ABC will beat this price by 10% so they will refund $100 + 10 = $110.

23. C
The purpose of this passage is to persuade.

24. B
The correct answer can be found in the fourth sentence of the first paragraph.

Choice A is incorrect because repenting begins the day AFTER Mardi Gras. Choice C is incorrect because you can celebrate Mardi Gras without being a member of a Krewe.

Choice D is incorrect because exploration does not play any

role in a modern Mardi Gras celebration.

25. A
The second sentence is the last paragraph states that Krewes are led by the Kings and Queens. Therefore, you must have to be part of a Krewe to be its King or its Queen.

Choice B is incorrect because it never states in the passage that only people from France can be Kings and Queen of Mardi Gras

Choice C is incorrect because the passage says nothing about having to speak French.

Choice D is incorrect because the passage does state that the Kings and Queens throw doubloons, which is fake money.

26. C
The first sentences of BOTH the 2nd and 3rd paragraphs mention that French explorers started this tradition in New Orleans.
Choices A, B and D are incorrect because they are names of cities or countries listed in the 2nd paragraph.

27. B
In the final paragraph, the word spectator is used to describe people who are watching the parade and catching cups, beads and doubloons.
Choices A and C are incorrect because we know the people who participate are part of Krewes. People who work the floats and parades are also part of Krewes

Choice D is incorrect because the passage makes no mention of people who do not celebrate Mardi Gras.

28. A
The 3 main emergency services are, the fire department, emergency medical and police

29. B
The main goals for the fire department are, to save lives, protect property and protect the environment.

30. B
The animal traditionally associated with firefighters are dalmatians.

Part II - Listening Comprehension

1. B
Household fires are so common because we use fire so often.

2. A
Most fires start in the kitchen.

3. B
Another major cause of fires is smoking.

8. C
The owners, Mary and John Smith went downtown for the day. Choice D is not mentioned at all, and can be eliminated right away. Choice B, visiting their friend upstairs, and choice C, are meant to confuse – the neighbor upstairs is mentioned in the news story, as the person that called them, but they were downtown at the time. Choices C is incorrect – the news story does mention they had breakfast, but it was not the cause of the fire.

9. A
Choice A, a candle left burning near some papers on a bookshelf is the correct answer. Choice B can be eliminated right away as it is not mentioned at all. The other choices, C and D are intended to distract. The neighbor and breakfast are mentioned, but not as the cause of the fire.

10. A
Yes their home burned down completely. From the story, "When Mary and John got home, the fire department had put out the fire, and there was only ashes."

11. B
Tom was going to school when he noticed the burning house.

12. B
Tom called the emergency services when he saw the house was on fire. From the passage, ". The teenager immediately called the emergency service and gave the address."

13. C
It took a long time for the fire department to arrive because the house was out of time

14. A
Most volcanoes are underwater

15. B
A split in the earth's plates causes volcanoes.

16. A
The volcano Vesuvius covered the city of Pompeii in minutes.

17. C
Shield volcanoes are common in the Hawaiian volcanic chain

18. B
Stratovolcanoes, which are tall conical mountains formed of lava flows

19. B
Underwater volcanoes do not have big explosions due to the weight of the water.

20. B
Mountains lions are found in Los Angeles backyards.

Part III – Mathematics

1. D
8327 – 1278 = 7049

2. B
294 X 21 = 6174

3. C
1278 + 4920 = 6198

4. A
285 * 12 = 3420

5. C
4120 – 3216 = 904

6. D
2417 + 1004 = 3421

7. B
1440 ÷ 12 = 120

8. C
2713 – 1308 = 1405

9. B
Formula for perimeter of a rectangle is 2(L + W)
The perimeter, p = 26, so 2(L+W) = p

The length is 5 inches more than the width, so

2(w+5) + 2w = 26
2w + 10 + 2w = 26
2w + 2w = 26 - 10
4w = 16

W = 16/4 = 4 inches

L is 5 inches more than w, so L = 5 + 4 = 9 inches.

11. D
Total cost of the items is $21,045 + $3,905 + $1,450 = $26,400
Total cost is now $26,400 + $5000 profit = $31,400

12. A
Number of mangos in the basket is 3/5 x 125 = 75
Number of ripe mangos = 2/5 x 75 = 30

13. D
The cost of the dishwasher = $450
15% discount amount = (450 * 15)/100 = $67.5
The discounted price = 450 − 67.5 = $382.5
20% additional discount amount on lowest price = (382.5 * 20)/100 = $76.5
So, the final discounted price = 382.5 - 76.5 = $306.00

14. D
Original price = x,
80/100 = 12590/X,
80X = 1259000,
X = 15737.50.

15. C
Total hay = 214 kg,
The goat eats at a rate of 214/60 days = 3.6 kg per day.
The Cow eats at a rate of 214/15 = 14.3 kg per day,
Together they eat 3.6 + 14.3 = 17.9 per day.
At a rate of 17.9 kg per day, they will consume 214 kg in 214/17.9 = 11.96 or 12 days approx.

16. A
25% = 25/100 = 1/4

17. C
125/100 = 1.25

18. D
40/100 = 30/X = 40X = 30*100 = 3000/40 = 75

19. B
12.5/100 = 50/X = 12.5X = 50 * 100 = 5000/12.5 = 400

20. C
24/56 = 3/7 (divide numerator and denominator by 8)

21. C
Converting percent to decimal − divide percent by 100 and remove the % sign. 87% = 87/100 = .87

22. A
60 has the same relation to X as 75 to 100 − so

60/X = 75/100
6000 = 75X
X = 80

23. D
60 has the same relationship to 100 as 12 does to X – so
60/100 = 12/X
1200 = 60X
X = 20

24. C
Converting a fraction to a decimal – divide the numerator by the denominator – so 71/1000 = .071. Dividing by 1000 moves the decimal point 3 places.

25. C
4.7 + .9 + .01 = 5.61

26. D
.84 ÷ .7 = 1.2

27. C
9 is in the ten thousandths place in 1.7389.

28. A
.87 - .48 = .39

29. C
1 foot = 12 inches, 60 feet = 60 x 12 = 720 inches.

30. A
1 centimeter = 10 millimeter, 25 centimeter = 25 X 10 = 250.

Part IV - Mechanical Aptitude

1. B
The smaller the distance between threads, the easier to turn.

2. C
75 pounds of force much be exerted downward on the rope to lift the 150 pound weight.

3. B
To solve for F, Weight X b (distance from fulcrum to weight) = Force X a (distance from fulcrum to point where force is applied)
100 X 5 = F X 10
500/10 = F
F =50

4. B
First calculate the speed of gear B. The gear ratio is 10:40 or 1:4. If gear A is turning at 80 rpm, then gear B, which is larger, will turn slower, 80/4 = 20 rpm.

Next calculate B and C. Gear C is smaller, so it will turn faster. The gear ratio is 40:10 or 4:1, and since gear B turns at 20 rpm, gear C will turn at 20 X 4 = 80 rpm.

Next calculate the direction. Gear A is turning clockwise, so Gear B is turning counter clockwise, so Gear C must be turning clockwise.

5. C
Notice the weight is attached to two of the pulleys. The weight required will therefore be 100/4 = 25 pounds.

6. B
A cam is a rotating or sliding piece in a mechanical linkage used especially in transforming rotary motion into linear motion or vice-versa

7. A
The function of the crankshaft is to transform the back-and-forth motion of the pistons into rotary motion.

8. B
The smaller gear will travel twice as fast as the larger gear.

9. A
A tachometer easures the rotation speed of a shaft, usualloy in a motor.

10. B
A hex key, Allen key, or Allen wrench (also known by various

other synonyms) is a tool of hexagonal cross-section (6-sided) used to drive bolts and screws that have a hexagonal socket in the head (internal-wrenching hexagon drive). [18]

11. A
A chuck is used to tighten bits in an electric drill.

12. C
There are three hydrants on Los Felix Blvd.

13. A
Taking the shortest route from Golden State Fwy 5 and Los Felix, to Santa Monica Blvd and Versont, there is one corner.

14. B
The width of the house from west to east is 37 feet.

15. C
The length of the house from north to south is 46 feet.

16. A
Choice B has the garage on the opposite side. Choice C does not have the indented front window beside the garage. Choice D has the front of the garage even with the front of the house.

17. A
Choice B is an entirely different house. Choice C is a different house the front porch extending out the front instead of inset. Choice D is the same house flipped horizontally.

18. C
The bottom box is rotated counter-clockwise.

19. C

20. D

21. B

22. D
Each figure has one more square with a cross inside.

23. C
Two large square boxes and one small square box are in-

verted.

24. B
Every box has three black square boxes inside.

25. D
The shape with empty inside circle has been rotated counter-clockwise.

Conclusion

CONGRATULATIONS! You have made it this far because you have applied yourself diligently to practicing for the exam and no doubt improved your potential score considerably! Getting into a good school is a huge step in a journey that might be challenging at times but will be many times more rewarding and fulfilling. That is why being prepared is so important.

Good Luck!

Practice Test Questions 2